The Holy Temple of Jerusalem

The Holy TEMPLE of Jerusalem

CHAIM RICHMAN

The Temple Institute
Carta, Jerusalem

Published by The Temple Institute & Carta, Jerusalem

Design: Alex Berlyne

Illustrations: The Temple Institute, Jerusalem
    Artists: Dmitry Baranovsky, George Berdichevsky, Shmu'el Lior,
        Leah Molokandov, Michael Putilov, Grigory Vechlis
   Craftsmen: Gadi Nataf and Chaim Odem (gold and silver vessels),
        Harrari Family (musical instruments)
  Photographs: Ya'acov Harlap

Reconstruction on page 92–3: Linn Ritmeyer

Maps on pages 8, 9, 91: Carta, Jerusalem

Plates: Reprocolor, Ltd., Tel Aviv

ISBN 965 – 220 – 359 – 9

Printed in Israel

Contents

Introduction

On the threshold of the third millennium, Jerusalem marks the 3,000th anniversary of the beginning of King David's reign, effectively establishing the city's Jewish roots. Though nearly 2,000 years have passed since the Second Temple was destroyed by the Roman legions, Jerusalem has remained the focal point of the Jewish people and the object of their yearning throughout all the long years of their exile.

The source of this longing, this great yearning for Jerusalem, can be found in the words of the prophet Isaiah (2:2–3): "And it shall come to pass in the last days, that the mountain of the Lord's house shall be established in the top of the mountains, and shall be exalted above the hills; and all nations shall flow unto it. And many people shall go and say, Come ye, and let us go up to the mountain of the Lord, to the house of the God of Jacob; and he will teach us of his ways, and we will walk in his paths: for out of Zion shall go forth the law, and the word of the Lord from Jerusalem." This belief—that the day would come when the entire world would live in harmony—recognizes Jerusalem as the spiritual center of all humanity.

Indeed, though the prophecy mentioned above refers to the end of days, when it will be fulfilled in its entirety, it was already partially realized in those ancient days. The First Temple, built by King Solomon (opposite), was widely acclaimed as one of the great wonders of the world, and during the era of the Second Temple, the teachings of great sages and leaders created a Golden Age. It was also in this era, during the reign of King Herod, that the sages of Israel were moved to record: "Whoever has not seen the Holy Temple built by King Herod, has never seen a beautiful building his entire life" (BT *Sukkah* 51:B).

The Jerusalem that houses the Holy Temple transcends its physical boundaries. Jerusalem is a concept. For the service in the Holy Temple is meant to be nothing less than an act of purification for all humanity. Through the ministrations of the priests and Levites, the participation of the Israelites, the pilgrimage of foreign nations, the sacrifice, the incense offering, the showbread, the menorah, and the Levite's song . . . each and every aspect is another note in a harmony of Divine orchestration. Within the Holy Temple, all forces unite to acknowledge Him who brought them all into being as the only reality, the Supreme Force which drives the universe. One of the most important principles of Jewish belief is that man has the capacity to engage in a direct, constant, and fulfilling relationship with his Creator. The memory of that relationship and the dream of its renewal keep the fires of the Temple altar burning within the collective heart of the nation of Israel, and the hearts of all those who cherish God and His message for humanity.

A story relates that Napoleon Bonaparte once entered a synagogue on Tisha B'Av, the solemn fast day that marks the anniversary of the destruction of the Holy Temple. Seeing the Jewish worshippers seated on the floor and reading Lamentations, he asked what terrible disaster had befallen them. He was told: "The Jews are in mourning for their Temple, Your Excellency."

"What Temple?" he asked. "When did this event occur?"

Upon learning that the Jews were grieving over the destruction of the Temple more than 1,700 years earlier, the emperor remarked: "Such a people as this will never be destroyed! If they still mourn for their Temple, they will surely see it rebuilt."

Psalm 30 was written by King David, who ordered it should be sung by the Levites during the dedication ceremonies of Solomon's Temple; some say that it was sung at the same event during the Second Temple, and that it will be sung at the dedication of the Third Temple as well.

I will extol thee, O Lord; for thou hast lifted me up, and hast not made my foes to rejoice over me.

O Lord my God, I cried unto thee, and thou hast healed me.

O Lord, thou hast brought up my soul from the grave: thou hast kept me alive, that I should not go down to the pit.

Sing unto the Lord, O ye saints of his, and give thanks at the remembrance of his holiness.

For his anger endureth but a moment; in his favour is life: weeping may endure for a night, but joy cometh in the morning.

And in my prosperity I said, I shall never be moved.

Lord, by thy favour thou hast made my mountain to stand strong: thou didst hide thy fact, and I was troubled.

I cried to thee, O Lord; and unto the Lord I made supplication.

What profit is there in my blood, when I go down to the pit? Shall the dust praise thee? shall it declare thy truth?

Hear, O Lord, and have mercy upon me: Lord, be thou my helper.

Thou hast turned for me my mourning into dancing: thou hast put off my sackcloth, and girded me with gladness;

To the end that my glory may sing praise to thee, and not be silent. O Lord my God, I will give thanks unto thee for ever.

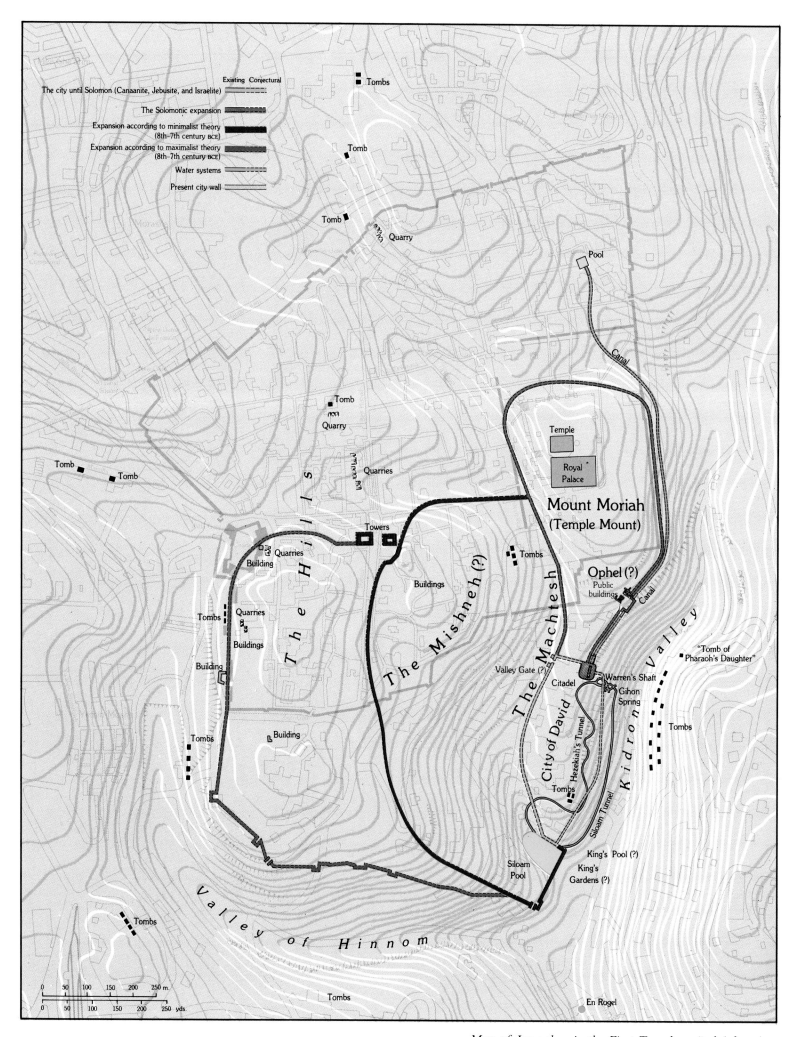

The city until Solomon (Canaanite, Jebusite, and Israelite)
The Solomonic expansion
Expansion according to minimalist theory (8th–7th century BCE)
Expansion according to maximalist theory (8th–7th century BCE)
Water systems
Present city wall

Existing Conjectural

Tombs

Tomb

Tomb

Quarry

Pool

Canal

Tomb

Quarry

Temple

Royal
Palace

Mount Moriah
(Temple Mount)

Tomb

Tomb

Quarries

Ophel (?)
Public
buildings

Canal

Towers

T h e   H i l l s

Quarries

Building

Buildings

Tombs

T
h
e

M
i
s
h
n
e
h

(
?
)

T
h
e

M
a
c
h
t
e
s
h

"Tomb of
Pharaoh's Daughter"

Tombs

Quarries

Buildings

Valley Gate (?)

Citadel

Warren's Shaft

Gihon
Spring

Building

City of David

Hezekiah's Tunnel

K
i
d
r
o
n

V
a
l
l
e
y

Tombs

Tombs

Building

Tombs

Siloam Tunnel

King's Pool (?)

Siloam
Pool

King's
Gardens (?)

V a l l e y   o f   H i n n o m

Tombs

0   50   100   150   200   250 m.
0   50   100   150   200   250 yds.

Tombs

En Rogel

*Map of Jerusalem in the First Temple period (above)
and Jerusalem in the Second Temple period (right).*

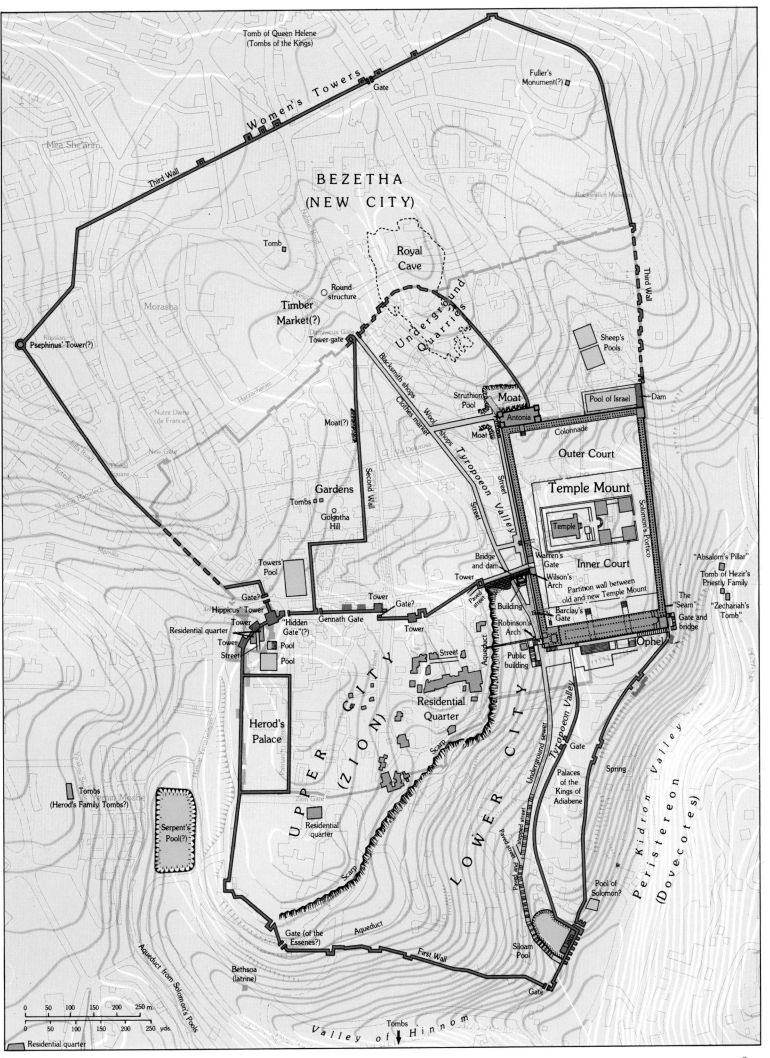

Tomb of Queen Helene
(Tombs of the Kings)

Fuller's
Monument(?)

Women's Towers

Gate

Third Wall

Rockefeller Museum

Mea She'arim

BEZETHA
(NEW CITY)

Tomb

Royal
Cave

Third Wall

Morasha

Round
structure

Timber
Market(?)

Underground Quarries

Russian
Psephinus' Tower(?)

Damascus Gate
Tower-gate

Sheep's
Pools

Notre Dame
de France

Blacksmith shops

Struthion
Pool

Moat

Pool of Israel

Dam

Jaffa Road

Moat(?)

Clothes market

Antonia

Moat

Colonnade

New Gate

Tzahal
Square

Via Dolorosa

Wool shops

Tyropoeon Valley

Street

Outer Court

Temple Mount

Gardens

Second Wall

Tombs

Golgotha
Hill

Street

Temple

Solomon's Portico

"Absalom's Pillar"

Towers'
Pool

Bridge
and dam

Warren's
Gate

Inner Court

Tomb of Hezir's
Priestly Family

Wilson's
Arch

Partition wall between
old and new Temple Mount

"Zechariah's
Tomb"

Gate?

Hippicus' Tower

Tower

"Hidden
Gate"(?)

Gennath Gate

Tower

Gate?

Paved
street

Building

Barclay's
Gate

The
"Seam"

Gate and
bridge

Tower

Tower

Street

Residential quarter

Robinson's
Arch

Tower

Ophel

Pool

Pool

U
P
P
E
R

Street

Residential
Quarter

Aqueduct

Public
building

Herod's
Palace

C
I
T
Y

Scarp

Gate

Palaces
of the
Kings of
Adiabene

Spring

Tombs
(Herod's Family Tombs?)

Yemin Moshe

(ZION)

Zion Gate

Residential
quarter

L
O
W
E
R

Underground sewer

Tyropoeon Valley

Peristereon
(Dovecotes)

Serpent's
Pool(?)

Scarp

C
I
T
Y

Paved street

stepped street
Paved
street

Pool of
Solomon?

Kidron Valley

Aqueduct from Solomon's Pools

Gate (of the
Essenes?)

Aqueduct

First Wall

Siloam
Pool

Gate

Bethsoa
(latrine)

0   50 100 150 200 250 m.

0   50 100 150 200 250 yds.

Tombs

Valley of Hinnom

Residential quarter

9

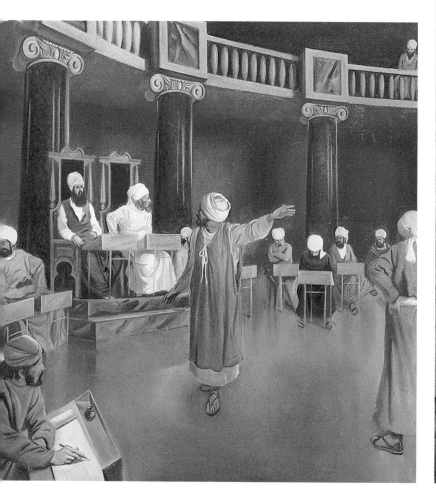

(above left) The members of the Sanhedrin meeting in the Chamber of Hewn Stone. Within the Holy Temple, the great sages of the Sanhedrin sat in a large semicircle, with the president in the center and the head of the rabbinical court at his right. The proceedings were recorded by the court scribes (left).

(above right) The Tabernacle in the wilderness surrounded by the Levite camp. The tent of Moses, facing the entrance to the Tabernacle, was the meeting place for the 70 elders, members of Moses' rabbinical court.

This chapter is exceptionally beautiful, and like many aspects of the Bible it can be interpreted on a variety of levels. But what does it have to do with the Holy Temple? In reality this psalm is a song of life which exemplifies the whole concept of the Holy Temple; it reflects its true purpose and nature, and contains within it the powerful secret of the Temple's role and function in the life of man, which is to dedicate the whole self to God, to elevate every aspect of the human experience to holiness and return the energy which He gives us to His service.

Since the Exodus, when the Israelites built the Tabernacle in the wilderness, the Temple has been the center of prophetic revelation, the royal authority of the Davidic and Hasmonean dynasties. It was the high point of all religious ceremony and the seat of the High Priest. Its Chamber of Hewn Stone was the convening place of the Sanhedrin, the legislative and judicial authority of the nation. From there, the knowledge of God spread to the entire world.

Twice the Temple was destroyed and the Jewish People

dispersed, yet the spirit of the Temple sustained them through bitter exile. It was Abraham who declared that the Temple of God would be established on Mount Moriah. King David laid the foundations and groundwork for building the Temple, and his son King Solomon erected it. And when the First Temple was destroyed and Israel was exiled to foreign shores, they remembered it by the rivers of Babylon.

Ezra and Nehemiah led 42,360 Jews back to Israel and immediately began to rebuild the Holy Temple. The Temple reached its height of splendor and magnificence during the reign of King Herod. Thus, over a period spanning nearly 1,000 years, the Holy Temple was the center of Jewish life. In our own days, the prophecy of redemption is being fulfilled before our eyes, stage by stage . . . with the ingathering of the exiles and the liberation of the Land.

In this work, we have tried to describe something of the world of the Holy Temple, with an emphasis on its centrality in everyday life. It would be a difficult task indeed to attempt to do justice to the vast amount of rich description and information preserved by the sages of Israel in the Oral Tradition, within the confines of a volume of this modest size and scope. Yet we have endeavored to cull from these sources as wide a range of events and details of Temple life as possible. It is our hope and prayer that this book may bring the reader to a greater appreciation of the Temple's historical significance, as well as its importance both for the Jewish people and the entire world. May we witness the realization of Haggai's prophecy (2:6–9): "For thus saith the Lord of hosts; Yet once, it is a little while, and I will shake the heavens, and the earth, and the sea, and the dry land; and I will shake all the nations, and the desire of all nations shall come: and I will fill this house with glory, saith the Lord of hosts. . . . The glory of this latter house shall be greater than of the former, saith the Lord of hosts: and in this place will I give peace, saith the Lord of hosts."

The Temple Sacrifices and Offerings

The significance and meaning of the Temple sacrificial system deserves an entire treatise in its own right. Sacrifice is prescribed by the Torah not only to atone for various minor sins but also on many other occasions. The present work is not the place for a lengthy treatment of this subject but as a great deal of misunderstanding exists as to the true purpose of the sacrifices, we present a brief introduction to the subject in an attempt to clarify a number of important points.

Animal sacrifice dates back to the most ancient times, Maimonides writes in the *Guide for the Perplexed*, having been a common form of worship from the earliest days of man's need for religious expression, and the Torah incorporated this type of practice by providing for such offerings. Sacrifices were among the earliest and most profound expressions of the human desire to come as close as possible to God. Thus the Bible records the sacrifices of Cain, Abel, and Noah.

As it existed in the Holy Temple, it functioned on many levels: ethical, moral, philosophical, mystical . . . and in fulfillment of the word of God. For although the idea of the sacrifices may seem difficult for contemporary man to accept, it is a Divine commandment.

Checking the definition of the word "sacrifice" in *Webster's Dictionary*, we begin to see a conceptual gap in our thinking which may explain much of the misunderstanding. In English the word "sacrifice" means something entirely different: **sac·ri·fice** 1: an act of offering something precious to deity; specifically, the offering of an immolated victim. 2: something offered in sacrifice. 3a: destruction or surrender of something for the sake of something else; 3b: something given up or lost {the —s made by parents}. 4: loss, deprivation.

However, the Hebrew word for "sacrifice" (*korban, le-hakriv*) is from the same root as "to come near, to approach . . . *to become closely involved in a relationship with someone.*" For this is meant to be the essence of the experience. Unfortunately, no word in the English language can adequately render the idea behind the Hebrew word *korban*. We use the word "sacrifice" for lack of a better word. The idea of a sacrifice or offering seems to indicate a gift or present; giving up something of value for another's benefit, or going without something of value yourself, for the benefit of another. None of this gift-giving idea, however, is present in the idea of the *korban*. First of all, it is a word which never carries a connotation of a present or gift, and is used exclusively by the Bible in the context of man's relationship with God. Thus its true meaning can only be grasped through its root . . . the concept of coming close. With this definition, the goal of the Temple sacrifices is nothing less than the aim of dedicating human life to a higher sphere of awareness . . . closer to the Creator and the source of all life. The Temple sacrifice is not an idea of giving something up or losing something of value; it strives for nearness to God. For as King David prayed in the Book of Psalms (73:28), "But it is good for me to draw near to God . . ."—for the Jew, nearness to God is the truest, the highest, the *only* conception of what goodness really is. Without this aspect to his life, without this Godly relationship which uplifts his physical existence and imbues his life with a sense of connection to the Divine, he feels himself to be like an animal, devoid of that which makes him into a human being. Without this he feels similar to the animal before him, on the altar. In a sense, what happens to the offering is also taking place within his heart and mind.

In the Temple service, all four aspects of creation unite together in the service of God, and thus reach their full potential in fulfilling His will and sanctifying His name. The priest who offers each sacrifice represents humanity; the animal offered, the animal kingdom; the flour, frankincense, libations, etc., represent the world of plants; and even the inanimate level is represented . . . for salt must be a part of every sacrifice. Thus when the Temple stands, all of creation functions in harmony. This is one aspect of how the Temple brings peace to the world: ". . . and in this place will I give peace, saith the Lord of hosts" (Haggai 2:9).

In all creation, man is unique because he is a living contradiction. He lives between the physical and spiritual worlds and, throughout his life, he is in constant struggle between the pull of these two opposing forces. His earthly body is the seat of the darker, physical nature which tries to pull him down, like gravity. His soul, which is the very part

(opposite) The High Priest offering incense upon the golden incense altar in the Sanctuary.

(left) The High Priest confessing over the bullock.

(right) The High Priest confessing over the scapegoat.

of Godliness itself, seeks to elevate him by subjugating his physical side to the spiritual.

When a sinner brought a *korban*, the offering showed him what he himself deserved, *were* God to judge him severely. The sages taught that we are able to have some knowledge of God and His identity through His names, or

Burning of the bullock and the goat for the sin offering: "And the bullock for the sin offering, and the goat for the sin offering, whose blood was brought in to make atonement in the holy place, shall one carry forth without the camp; and they shall burn in the fire their skins, and their flesh, and their dung" (Lev. 16:27).

attributes. Throughout the Book of Leviticus, God never refers to Himself with the Name *Elohim* in reference to the *korbanot*-offerings, which denotes the Divine attribute of strict justice. This could be misconstrued to indicate that God is a vengeful, bloodthirsty deity who demands a sacrifice as reparation. But nothing could be further from the truth; such imagery is a heathen vision of God, an unforgiving God who accepts the death throes of an animal as a substitute for the forfeited life of a human being. But the only Name which the Bible associates with the offerings to God is *HaShem*, YHWH—the attribute of Divine love and mercy.

Precisely because He is the God of love, not the God of punishment and death, He has prepared the sacrificial

system as a method of restoring and purifying man's moral and spiritual life. The sacrifice represents the death of man's physical side, the side of him that will die when kept from God, but if he will bring his entire self into His service, he will connect with his true purpose, the strengthening of his spiritual nature through the denial of his own animal urges. Thus he gives satisfaction to his Creator; the "pleasing aroma" of the sacrifices is the product of this purification.

The experience of bringing this sacrifice gives him a vicarious taste of death, and reconciles his animal and spiritual natures.

The sacrifices were not an end in themselves. The sin offering, which was only a small part of all the Temple sacrifices, was not acceptable unless it was accompanied by true repentance. We are likewise taught that God Himself required the sacrifice for the betterment of the crown of His creation, man; however, He would prefer that man not sin, and then no offering would be necessary (BT *Berakoth* 22:A).

The revulsion felt by those who refer disparagingly to the "cult" of Temple sacrifice is understandable, since they view the sacrificial system as brutal. They have no conception of a God who commands us to raise ourselves above the animals and dedicate ourselves to Him. For man is at the center of creation; all else which God created was brought into existence solely to help aid man in his quest for spiritual perfection.

The Priests

And thou shall anoint them . . . for their anointing shall surely be an everlasting priesthood throughout their generations.

(Ex. 40:15)

For the Lord thy God hath chosen him out of all thy tribes, to stand to minister in the name of the Lord, him and his sons for ever.

(Deut. 18:5)

The first *kohen*, the founder of the priestly clan, was Aaron, brother of Moses, of the tribe of Levi. All Israel is descended from the 12 sons of Jacob whose third son was Levi. Aaron, a fourth generation descendant of Levi, and his four sons were designated as the first priests. He served as the first High Priest and all of his male descendants were chosen by God to be priests forever; it is an eternal covenant. Thus even today, a *kohen* is a direct descendant of Aaron.

The Holy One chose these men to be spiritual leaders. Thus a *kohen* is called upon to direct himself, and others, in the proper service of God: "And take thou unto thee Aaron thy brother, and his sons with him, from among the children of Israel, that he may minister unto me in the priest's office . . ." (Ex. 28:1).

The reader is undoubtedly most familiar with the primary role which the priests performed in the Temple, that of officiating at the sacrifices and other parts of the service. No less important was their function as a conduit bringing God's radiant blessing and influence into this world. It is on this account that they were commanded to deliver God's blessing of peace and love to the people, as well: "Speak unto Aaron and unto his sons, saying, On this wise ye shall bless the children of Israel, saying unto them, The Lord bless thee, and keep thee: The Lord make his face shine upon thee, and be gracious unto thee: The Lord lift up his countenance upon thee, and give thee peace" (Num. 6:23–26).

It is the one original aspect of Temple worship mandated by the Bible which is still performed to this day. In most places in Israel, priests recite this blessing in their respective congregations daily; in the Diaspora, however, many congregations invoke the priestly blessing only on the major holidays.

(opposite) The King of Israel reading aloud from the Torah scroll to the people gathered in the Holy Temple at the end of Sukkot.

"They [the priests] must be holy unto their God. . . . Thou shalt sanctify him therefore; for he offereth the bread of thy God; he shall be holy unto thee: for I the Lord, which sanctify you, am holy" (Lev. 21:6–8).

Many people equate the concept of holiness with spirituality in general; anything ethereal or mystical is presumed to be holy. This is a serious misconception, for *holy* and *spiritual* are not the same thing, and they are certainly not equal. Many people, disciplines, philosophies and the like may be considered spiritual in nature; they may concern themselves with the esoteric; they may even occupy themselves with the service of God—but this does not necessarily imply that they are *holy* in any way. In fact, some spiritual paths can most definitely be the absolute epitome of *unholiness*.

The Bible is clear in its prohibition of spiritualism which has not been authorized by God. "Ye shall not eat any thing with the blood: neither shall ye use enchantment, nor observe times" (Lev. 19:26), we are warned. These forbidden practices include superstitious omens and astrology. When the children of Israel were preparing to enter the Promised Land, they were specifically warned by God to uproot the perverted spiritual practices of its former inhabitants. "When the Lord thy God shall cut off the nations from before thee, whither thou goest to possess them, and thou succeedest them, and dwellest in their land; take heed to thyself that thou be not snared by following them, after that they be destroyed from before thee; and that thou inquire not after their gods, saying, How did these nations serve their gods? even so will I do likewise. Thou shalt not do so unto the Lord thy God: for every abomination to the Lord, which he hateth, have they done unto their gods; for even their sons and their daughters they have burnt in the fire to their gods" (Deut. 12:29–31).

In contrast to the concept of "spiritual," the primary definition of "holy" is "*set apart* to the service of God."

God Himself is called holy because He is completely separate, unique and unequalled in all of His creation. Nothing can be compared to Him because He is peerless; He is the Creator of the universe and all existence, and absolutely different from anything else that exists.

It is in this light that Israel is collectively called upon to be a "holy nation," that is, a nation set apart from all others, completely different from any other, living proof that an entire nation can walk with God in its midst: ". . . lo, the people shall dwell alone, and shall not be reckoned among the nations" (Num. 23:9). This separation is the true holiness. To be holy is to be removed from the realm of the ordinary. Israel lives separately, according to the Torah's commandments, precisely because God is separate . . . for the highest form of religious experience is to reflect, to imitate the Divine. Man is a reflection of his Creator.

So too, the priests in the Holy Temple "must be holy . . . for I the Lord am holy." If Jewish life is to be holy, then the priests must take care to be especially holy. They have been singled out by the Creator Himself for all time to devote their lives to Him.

In tractate *Midot*, we are taught that the offices of the Sanhedrin, the supreme body of judicial legislation, were located on the southern side of the court and were constructed of square hewn stones.

In describing the location of the Chamber of Hewn Stone, the Talmud points out that it was built in such a fashion that half was within the sanctified area of the Temple Mount complex and half was outside, in the unsanctified portion. It was in this second half that the Sanhedrin held court. Here, the members sat in a large semi-circle and spread, through the wisdom of their teachings and decisions, knowledge of God and His Torah throughout all Israel. Here they also examined candidates for the priesthood. This was an affair which occupied them constantly. It was necessary to consider each priest according to the regulations and stipulations of biblical law, in order to determine if each man was free from blemishes and any of the other disqualifications and therefore fit to serve in the Temple. The Levites were judged and examined in the same manner.

On those occasions when the Sanhedrin failed to find one priestly candidate who was unfit, the day was marked with great rejoicing and celebration, and they would declare:

Blessed be the Holy One! Blessed is He!
For no blemish has been found amongst the descendants of Aaron.
And blessed is He who has chosen Aaron and his offspring to stand
in service before the Lord, in the holiest of places.

(*Midot* 5,4)

The *kohanim* who were responsible for the daily service in the Holy Temple were divided into 24 separate shifts made up of men who hailed from all parts of the land. The duration of each shift's duties was for one week, when they would be entirely responsible for all of the daily functions in the Temple. Rather like military reservists, each priest would be expected to perform his obligatory period of service in the Temple. The shifts were further divided into six clans, or family branches, each serving for one day, but on the Sabbath all six clans worked together.

All wanted the opportunity to conduct the Divine services but these were only a specific number of daily tasks, and it was impossible for everyone to attend to these at once. In order to give each priest an equal opportunity to officiate, special lotteries were held each day and the members of the family clan who were serving that day would participate in this drawing.

Four separate drawings were held daily and thus the courtyard was filled with the priests a number of times throughout the day. Before the first lottery, all the priests who were eligible would purify themselves in a *mikvah*, a special pool of naturally collected water. This immersion was necessary for everyone, even for a priest who was certain that he had not become defiled. The priests would

The High Priest swearing an oath to the Sanhedrin elders that he will not deviate from anything that he had been taught. This took place in the chamber of the Avtinas family, where the incense for the Temple service was prepared.

then make their way to the Chamber of Hewn Stone where the lotteries took place and which was partially in the holy area. The drawing took place in a circle. A number would be picked and agreed upon, substantially higher than the number of men present. The overseer would then declare that each man present raise a finger. Then, each finger would be counted (since the Bible forbids the counting of actual people: see Ex. 30:12), moving throughout the circle over and over again until reaching the number that had been pre-selected.

After the winner of the first lottery had been determined, the priests divided into two separate columns. This dawn patrol was responsible for checking that everything in the Temple was in order, that nothing had been disturbed during the night, and that all of the 93 sacred vessels which were needed to perform the Divine service were in their proper place.

Each column of the priestly patrol was led by a

torchbearer except on the Sabbath nights when their way was lit by candles. One group went eastward, and transversed the northern and eastern sections of the colonnade; the second group walked westward, crossing a small portion of the northern side, plus the entire western and southern sides, and a short distance on the east. They continued their patrol until they met up with each other at the Chamber of the Meal-Offering Preparation, where the High Priest's daily meal offerings were kneaded and baked. This chamber was in the eastern sector of the court, south of the Nikanor Gates. They then greeted each other, if nothing had been found amiss, with the words "Peace! All is peaceful!"

Before leaving the Chamber of the Meal-Offering Preparation, the priests left several of their number there to begin readying the High Priest's meal offering.

The first of the daily lotteries determined which priest

As the sacrifice was being offered upon the altar, a priest (left)
would pour out the wine libation into a silver cup while the overseer
(center) would signal to the Levitical choir to begin the daily song.

would carry out the removal of ashes from the altar, around which all of the Divine service was centered, including the Passover sacrifice, the bringing of the first-fruits on Shavuot and the rejoicing with *lulav* branches on Sukkot.

Both the altar of Solomon's Temple and that of Herod's were on the same site, on Mount Moriah, where Abraham had bound Isaac. It was built as a perfect square and was quite large, reaching a height of 10 *amot* (approximately five meters) and its width was 32 *amot* (approximately 16 meters). There were two main parts: the altar itself, and the ascent ramp. Both were constructed of stones and earth. On top of the altar, at its four corners, there were hollow boxes which made small protrusions or "horns." These horns each measured one *amah* square and five handbreadths high (or approximately 18 x 18 x 15 inches).

Three separate piles of wood burned atop the altar. The largest was designated to receive all the sacrifices; the second provided the coals for the incense altar within the sanctuary; and the third was the "perpetual fire." "The fire shall ever be burning upon the altar; it shall never go out" (Lev. 6:13). The ashes from the altar were removed to another location outside the Holy Temple which was known as the "place of ashes."

"And the Lord spake unto Moses, saying, Command Aaron and his sons, saying, This is the law of the burnt offering: It is the burnt offering, because of the burning upon the altar all night unto the morning, and the fire of the altar shall be burning in it. And the priest shall put on his linen garment, and his linen breeches shall he put upon his flesh, and take up the ashes which the fire hath consumed with the burnt offering on the altar, and he shall put them beside the altar. And he shall put off his garments, and put on other garments, and carry forth the ashes without the camp unto a clean place" (Lev. 6:8–11).

The priest charged with removing the ashes was forbidden to "touch the vessel until after you have sanctified your hands and feet from the water of the laver!" The vessel referred to was the silver shovel which was used especially for the purpose of removing the ashes. It was forbidden to begin any sacred Temple service (or even to draw near to the altar) until the priest had "sanctified" his hands and feet at the laver. "For Aaron and his sons shall wash their hands and their feet thereat: when they go into the tabernacle of the congregation, they shall wash with water, that they die not; or when they come near to the altar to minister, to burn offering made by fire unto the Lord: so they shall wash their hands and their feet, that they die not: and it shall be a statute for ever to them, even to him and to his seed throughout their generations" (Ex. 30:19–21).

No one could accompany the priest as he entered the hall that led into the Holy Temple's interior. Entrance to the area between the hall and the altar or its ramp was forbidden to all but the priest who was engaged in performing the service. Making his way solely by the light of the fire that burned atop the altar, he could not be seen by his colleagues once he entered the hall and approached the copper laver which stood on the western side of the altar. When he reached the laver, the others finally knew his position, not by sight but by sound, for they could hear the "*muchni* of Ben Katin," the sound of a wooden wheel especially devised by Ben Katin, one of the High Priests of the Second Temple. This mechanism was a large pulley which lowered the laver into a well at night, and pulled it

A priest pours out the libation and his colleague adjusts the fire atop the altar while other priests below blow their trumpets as the Israelites look on.

up in the morning filled with water.

Once the officiating priest had purified himself, he took the silver shovel from its spot and walked up the ramp, ascending to the top of the altar. He collected some of the ashes and took them to the Place of Ashes, on the eastern side of the ramp.

Once the first priest had removed the small amount of ashes, the other priests could now attend to the more general preparation of the altar, gathering together any parts of the sacrifices which had not been burned to ashes during the night and moving them to the sides of the altar (since it is forbidden to remove any part of a sacrifice from atop the altar).

Following the raking of the ashes, the next task was to bring new wood up to the altar for the large fire. After both the large arrangement and the smaller one for the incense had been lit, the priests descended from the altar and returned to the Chamber of Hewn Stone for the second lottery.

Returning to the Chamber of Hewn Stone after the wood piles had been arranged atop the altar, the priests once again gathered for the second daily lottery. This drawing would determine the distribution of a number of various assignments pertaining to the sacrifice and offering of the *tamid*, the daily sacrifice: which priest would slaughter the sacrifice; who would collect its blood and dash it upon the altar; who would remove the excess ash from the inner (golden) incense altar within the sanctuary; who would attend to the wicks of the menorah, cleansing the cups of used oil and ash; which six priests would bring the parts of the sacrifice to the altar's ramp; who would bring the fine flour for the accompanying meal offering up to the altar; who would bring up the High Priest's meal offering; and who would pour the wine libation.

Immediately following the lottery, the priests chosen to remove the ashes from the incense altar and to attend to the menorah prepared themselves and the vessels required to carry out their respective services. These vessels were a golden basket which held 2 1/2 *kavim* (about 5 1/2 liters); an oil container, shaped like a large wine goblet and also fashioned of gold; and two keys. They gave these keys to the Levite gatekeeper on duty; the Levites were entrusted with guarding all the Temple gates. The Levite who was appointed to open the Sanctuary took these keys from the priests and, opening the small door to the right, entered first into an antechamber and then into the area of the Sanctuary itself. Reaching the great gates, he removed the door-bolt and the locks and opened wide the gates.

The act of opening the Sanctuary gates had great significance, for the morning *tamid* sacrifice could not be prepared for offering upon the altar until they had been opened. In fact, the priest who had been assigned to this task would not commence until *he actually heard the sound of the great gates opening.*

The overseer then declared to the priests: "Let one go up to a high place in the Temple, to see whether the time has arrived to offer the morning sacrifice!" If the night had indeed begun to wane, the watchman cried out "*Barkai!* The day has dawned!" Then the priests waited for the second announcement when he in the high place would call out, "The entire eastern horizon is illuminated." Once the eastern sky began to lighten, one of those down below called up to his colleague: "Does the glow extend all the way to Hebron?"

If the watchman answered "Yes," the proper time had come for offering the *tamid* daily sacrifice, and the gates of the Sanctuary were opened. The overseer instructed the priests who would be in attendance, "Bring a lamb from the Chamber of Lambs!" At all times a minimum of six animals previously checked and certified as blemish-free were kept for the daily sacrifices.

Although the lamb which had been selected for the *tamid* sacrifice had already been ascertained as being free of any disqualifying blemish, it was checked again by torchlight, after its removal from the chamber. After it had been selected, the lamb was given a drink from a golden vessel before it was slaughtered, for this made its skin easier to remove.

After selecting a lamb from the Chamber of Lambs, the *kohanim* entered into the Chamber of Vessels, where the Temple vessels were stored. There, they removed all the 93 sacred vessels of silver and gold which were required for the Divine service during the course of the day.

The priest who had won first place in the lottery, and thus the right to slaughter the *tamid*, led the lamb to the area of the court north of the altar. He was followed by the six priests who would carry the parts of the sacrifice up to the altar's ramp. This area was especially equipped with metal rings in the floor for holding the animals, eight small stone columns, topped with wooden blocks and fitted with metal rings for removing the skin, and marble tables for preparing the sacrifices to be brought to the altar.

The priest assigned to remove the incense altar's ashes now entered the Sanctuary, straight through the open gates carrying the golden basket and made his way into the holy place. Standing before the golden incense altar, he first placed the basket down, on the Sanctuary floor. Then he removed the ashes from the incense altar into the palms of his hands, and put them in the basket before him. When only a small amount of ashes were left over, he used a small brush to sweep them into the basket. Then he left the basket on the floor before him, to be removed later on in the service.

At the same time, the colleague who had been assigned the next task entered the Sanctuary and approached the menorah, which stood on the south side, the golden seven-branched candlestick that is described in the Book of Exodus: "And thou shalt make a candlestick of pure gold: of beaten work shall the candlestick be made: his shaft, and his branches, his bowls, his knops, and his flowers, shall be of the same. And six branches shall come out of the sides of it; three branches of the candlestick out of the one side, and three branches of the candlestick out of the other side: Three bowls made like unto almonds, with a knop and a flower in one branch; and three bowls made like almonds in the other branch, with a knop and a flower: so in the six branches that come out of the candlestick. And in the candlestick shall be four bowls made like unto almonds, with their knops, and their flowers. And there shall be a knop under two branches of the same. . . . Their knops and their branches shall be of the same: all it shall be one beaten work of pure gold. And thou shalt make the seven lamps thereof: and they shall light the lamps thereof, that they may give light over against it" (Ex. 25:31–37).

This priest removed the spent wicks and oil from the individual lamps, prepared new ones, and replenished the full measure of oil for each light. In order to accomplish this task, the priest ascended the three marble steps which stood in front of the menorah. These corresponded to

three biblical verses which mention "going up" in relation to the menorah:

"And the Lord spake unto Moses, saying, Speak unto Aaron, and say unto him, When thou lightest the lamps, the seven lamps shall *give light over against the candlestick*" (Num. 8:1–2).

"And thou shalt make the seven lamps thereof: and they shall light the lamps thereof, that they may *give light over against it*" (Ex. 25:37).

"And thou shalt command the children of Israel, that they bring thee pure oil olive beaten for the light, *to cause the lamp to burn always*" (Ex. 27:20).

At this point, the *tamid* daily sacrifice was slaughtered, and the next six priests drawn by the lottery brought various parts of the sacrifice up to the altar ramp. The seventh priest brought the fine flour for the meal offering that acccompanied the daily sacrifice.

The eighth priest would bring the High Priest's personal meal offering up to the altar. This consisted of 1/10 of an *ephah* (approximately two quarts) of flour which had been mixed with oil in a pan and baked into 12 loaves. Although this was the High Priest's own, it was considered in many ways like a congregational offering. Incidentally, this offering was also brought by every priest who began to officiate in the Temple, on the first day of his service, as part of his inauguration ceremony. The ordinary, or lay priests only brought it on the day they took office, but the High Priest would bring this offering every day: "And the Lord spake unto Moses, saying, This is the offering of Aaron and of his sons, which they shall offer unto the Lord in the day when he is anointed; the tenth part of an ephah of fine flour for a meat offering perpetual, half of it in the morning, and half thereof at night" (Lev. 6:19–20).

Once all the parts of the sacrifice, and the meal offering, had been placed on the altar, they were salted, as God commanded: ". . . with all thine offerings thou shalt offer salt" (Lev. 2:13).

Finally, the last priest in this lottery received the task of bringing the 1/4 *hin* (approximately one quart) measurement of wine which was poured upon the altar for the morning wine libation that accompanied the daily sacrifice. Thus, a total of 13 priests were appointed in the second daily lottery. The entire staff needed for the daily sacrifice was now in place, and after these priests had concluded their tasks, they returned to the Chamber of Hewn Stone for the recitation of their morning prayers. Here, the lottery overseer would tell the priests that it was time to recite the "Hear O Israel" prayer, together with its corresponding blessing. They also recited the Ten Commandments, since these embodied the main principles of the Torah.

After both the daily sacrifice and the incense offering were concluded, the priests would raise their hands and deliver the "priestly blessing" upon the congregation of Israel assembled in the Holy Temple. On the Sabbath, an extra blessing was added, with which the outgoing shift of priests greeted the incoming one: "May He who causes His Name to dwell in this House, cause love, brotherhood, peace and friendship to dwell among you."

The third lottery was unique. This was held to determine who would have a chance to officiate at the incense offering, which, according to Jewish tradition, was the most acceptable part of the Temple service in God's eyes; it was influential in subduing evil, and its characteristic quality

Priests bringing portions of the sacrifice up the ramp to the top of the altar, where they are placed on the fire.

(opposite page) Priest attending the lamp, replacing and relighting the wicks, and replenishing the oil.

aided in amplifying the aspect of Divine mercy and benevolence in the world.

"And thou shalt make an altar to burn incense upon; of shittim wood shalt thou make it. A cubit shall be the length thereof, and a cubit the breadth thereof; four-square shall it be: and two cubits shall be the height thereof: the horns thereof shall be the same. And thou shalt overlay it with pure gold, the top thereof, and the sides thereof round about, and the horns thereof; and thou shalt make unto it a crown of gold round about.

"And two golden rings shalt thou make to it under the crown of it, by the two corners thereof, upon the two sides of it shalt thou make it; and they shall be for places for the staves to bear it withal. And thou shalt make the staves of shittim wood, and overlay them with gold.

"And thou shalt put it before the vail that is by the ark of the testimony, before the mercy seat that is over the testimony, where I will meet with thee. And Aaron shall burn thereon sweet incense every morning: when he dresseth the lamps, he shall burn incense upon it. And when Aaron lighteth the lamps at even, he shall burn incense upon it, a perpetual incense before the Lord throughout your generations.

"Ye shall offer no strange incense thereon, nor burnt sacrifice, nor meat offering; neither shall ye pour drink offering thereon. And Aaron shall make an atonement upon the horns of it once in a year with the blood of the sin offering of atonements: once in the year shall he make atonement upon it throughout your generations: it is most holy unto the Lord" (Ex. 30:1–10).

The fourth daily lottery was held with the participation of all priests to determine who would bring the parts of the sacrifice from the altar's ramp up to the top, where the sacrifices were consumed in the altar's fire. The priest chosen would place the portions on the altar's fire, and pour out the accompanying libation. He would then prepare the special vessels of the incense service: a large golden spoon which held the amount of 3 *kavim*, and a smaller vessel, filled to the brim with the incense and placed inside the larger vessel to prevent any of the incense from spilling.

It was also the turn of the priest who had been assigned to gather the coals for the inner altar, to bring the silver shovel and climb to the top of the outer altar, where he would rake and collect some of the coals. Having descended with the coals, he transferred them into a golden shovel which he would take into the Sanctuary for the incense service.

The priest who would offer the incense would make his way toward the Sanctuary together with the one who bore the shovel, but, before arriving there, in between the hall and the altar, one of them would take a vessel called a *magrepha* and throw it down to the floor! This signal served three purposes:

1. When the priests who were outside the court heard the sound, they knew that their colleagues within were about to prostrate themselves before the Divine Presence and they ran to bow down with them.

2. When the Levites heard it, they knew that the Levite choir was about to enter the court and stand upon the platform, to begin their service of the daily song. They, too, ran to join their brothers.

3. And when the assembly head (the official in charge of the Israelites who represented the entire people at the sacrificial service) heard it, he separated the priests who had become defiled, and stood them all together at the Eastern Gate. This way, everyone could see that they were impure and therefore could not serve in the Holy Temple, and no one would suspect that they had any other reason for not participating in the service.

The two priests now continued up the 12 steps that led to the Sanctuary, preceded by two other priests—those whose task it was to remove the residue ashes from both the inner (incense) altar, and the menorah. Using the edges of the shovel, the first would arrange the coals upon the altar evenly, so that the incense would burn well. He then took the basket which he left there earlier, prostrated himself and left, having concluded his task.

The second then entered, and if he found the two easternmost candles still burning, he extinguished the outside flame so that he could replenish its oil, replace its wick and then relight it. He did not extinguish the "western candle," the second flame from the end—this "perpetual flame" he allowed to burn continuously and from this he rekindled the menorah in the evening.

If the "western candle" had gone out, he cleansed its lamp as well, replenished its oil and wick, and rekindled its light from the fire atop the outer altar. Afterwards, he took up the vessel containing the burned wicks and other waste which he had left on the second step, prostrated himself once, and left the Sanctuary.

The priest who attended to the incense service now entered the Sanctuary, together with an assistant. He removed the smaller vessel filled with incense, and handed it to his assistant who would place some of the incense in the priest's palms. Officiating at the incense service only happened once in each priest's life, so he had been warned that he must be very cautious when placing the incense upon the burning coals. If he sprinkled it on the coals too close to the side where he was standing, he would be burned, so he was instructed to sprinkle it away from himself.

Upon receiving word from the overseer that he might now begin, the priest began to let the grains fall slowly from his palms across the top of the altar and when the entire chamber filled with the cloud of incense, he prostrated himself and left the Sanctuary.

After the priests had concluded their sacred duties within the Sanctuary, they bowed down and left the Sanctuary, to stand upon the 12 steps which led down to the area before the altar.

The priests who attended to the inner altar's ashes, the menorah's wick, the shovel, and the incense, all stood to the right of their colleagues (who had brought the parts of the sacrifice up to the altar). They held all the vessels they had been using in their service: the golden baskets which held the ashes and wicks, the shovel and the incense utensils. Now they put these vessels down and turned to face the congregation, extended their hands and recited the Priestly Blessing: "The Lord bless thee, and keep thee: The Lord make his face shine upon thee, and be gracious unto thee: The Lord lift up his countenance upon thee, and give thee peace" (Num. 6:24–26).

(opposite) Priest sprinkling incense in front of the golden altar.

(above) Preparing the ashes of the red heifer for the purification of all those arriving at the Temple. The heifer was slaughtered on an altar on the Mount of Anointment, opposite the Temple Mount. Cedar wood, hyssop and crimson wool were placed into the fire, and the procedure was overseen by a large assembly, including the elders of Israel.

(right) A priest using a sprig of hyssop to purify those who had become ritually unclean. After dipping the branch into a solution of pure water and ashes, the priest sprinkles the solution onto a father and son who had been exposed to impurity.

Purity in the Temple

It is difficult for contemporary man to understand what was known as "ritual purity" and its opposite, "ritual impurity," in the time of the Temple, terms which it is impossible to translate precisely. This purity, or lack of it, has no connection with physical cleanliness. It is a spiritual state that can be caused by a variety of factors. The most severe form of all is brought on by exposure to death; indeed, although there are many types of impurity, the state which Torah law is most commonly concerned with is generally associated with some aspect of death. One who is impure is forbidden contact with anything holy and cannot enter a sanctified area until he undergoes purification by being sprinkled with the ashes of the red heifer. Impurity indicates a spiritual imbalance, and the Temple is the place which restores this balance.

While the priests had to guard against any form of defilement, they had to excercise particular care to avoid contact with the most stringent form of impurity of all, exposure to death. They were commanded not to become defiled "by the dead among his people," with the exception of the close blood relatives who are specified. The High Priest was forbidden to come into contact even with these.

Just what is it about death that causes such impurity? Is it a remnant of some deep-rooted, tribal taboo, a superstitious practice recalling the earliest, most base and primordial of man's fears? Nothing could be further from the truth. While the heathen paid tribute to the gods of death who claimed everything and everyone as their own, Judaism is a celebration of life.

The priests were primarily emissaries of the one God who manifests Himself by giving life and the promise of eternal life. Once life has departed, it is not the stuff of death itself which renders impurity, but the absence of God-given life. As long as man has free will, and lives in accordance with his Creator's will, he creates eternal life from death, and proves that death is not the end, but merely a graduation. What men call "death" is nothing more than the bonds of transitory life giving way to eternal life. But in our limited vision and understanding, we view this bleakly and oppressively as death. It is a myopic outlook, but it is also a facet of the human condition that cannot be undone until the day that "He will swallow up death in victory; and the Lord God will wipe away tears from off all faces . . ." (Isa. 25:8).

Moreover, because of the elevated status of the priests, a status which raises them aloft of the flitting shadows of ephemeral, earthly death, they are commanded: "They shall not make baldness upon their head . . . nor make any cuttings in their flesh" (Lev. 21:5). Faced with death, the ancients sought to make atonement by self-mutilation, a tribute to the god of death.

Several methods of restoring purity were used in the Holy Temple, most notably immersion in water, but the Bible's exclusive remedy for defilement caused by exposure to death was sprinkling with the ashes of the red heifer. Many of the thousands who arrived at the Holy Temple had to undergo this process before they could enter into the court.

"And the Lord spake unto Moses and unto Aaron, saying, This is the ordinance of the law which the Lord hath commanded, saying, Speak unto the children of Israel, that they bring thee a red heifer without spot, wherein is no blemish . . . and ye shall give her unto Eleazar the priest . . . and one shall slaughter her before his face. . . . And shall burn the heifer in his sight . . . and it shall be kept for the congregation of the children of Israel for a water of separation: it is a purification for sin . . . and it shall be unto the children of Israel, and unto the stranger that sojourneth among them, for a statute for ever" (Num. 19:1–10).

The heifer must be three years old, "perfect in its redness," totally free from any physical blemish or defect, whether internal or external. Furthermore, it must never have carried a burden or been harnessed a yoke or plough.

There is a tradition which connects the concept of the red heifer with the sin of the golden calf which Israel, under the influence of the Mixed Multitude, committed in the desert 40 days after the revelation at Mount Sinai, and it must be red, on account of the verse which promises "though your sins be as scarlet . . ." (Isa. 1:18), for sin is alluded to as "red."

The heifer was prepared on the Mount of Anointment, on the Mount of Olives, directly opposite the eastern entrance to the Sanctuary. After slaughtering the heifer, the priest sprinkled its blood seven times while facing the Temple. Afterwards, the heifer burned on a pile of cedar and hyssop wood, tied together by a scarlet band. A small amount of the ashes was placed in a vessel containing natural spring water and this was sprinkled with a branch of hyssop onto the body of anyone who had become impure.

On the seventh day after the sprinkling, the individual would then immerse himself in the waters of a *mikvah*.

The Priestly Garments

Moses was instructed by God that the garments of the priests were to be both dignified and beautiful, as precious as the garments of royalty.

"And take thou unto thee Aaron thy brother, and his sons with him, from among the children of Israel, that he may minister unto me in the priest's office, even Aaron, Nadab and Abihu, Eleazar and Ithamar, Aaron's sons. And thou shalt make holy garments for Aaron thy brother for glory and for beauty. And thou shalt speak unto all that are wise hearted, whom I have filled with the spirit of wisdom, that they may make Aaron's garments to consecrate him, that he may minister to me in the priest's office. And these are the garments which they shall make; a breastplate, and an ephod, and a robe, and a broidered coat, a mitre, and a girdle: and they shall make holy garments for Aaron thy brother, and his sons, that he may minister unto me in the priest's office" (Ex. 28:1–4).

Why does the Bible attach so much significance to the garments? Because they possess a certain holiness, powerful enough to sanctify all those who merely came in contact with them: ". . . and they shall not sanctify the people with their garments" (Ezek. 44:19).

The priestly garments were not *sewn* but *woven* in one piece, without seams. The only exception was the sleeves of the robe, which were woven separately and then sewn onto the robe.

There were three categories of priestly garments: (1) the High Priest's apparel that was worn all year round, consisting of eight garments called the "golden garments"; (2) the clothing worn by the High Priest on the Day of Atonement, which consisted of four garments called the "white garments"; and (3) the uniform of the ordinary priests, consisting of four garments.

The eight garments worn by the High Priest all year round were the ephod, breastplate, robe, a broidered coat, mitre, girdle, plate, and breeches, as described in the Book of Exodus: "And these are the garments which they shall make; a breastplate, and an ephod, and a robe, and a broidered coat, a mitre, and a girdle . . ." (Ex. 28:4); "And you shalt make a plate of pure gold . . ." (ibid. v. 36); "And thou shalt make them linen breeches" (ibid. v. 42).

On the Day of Atonement, the Bible states, "He [the High Priest] shall put on the holy linen coat, and he shall have the linen breeches upon his flesh, and shall be girded with a linen girdle, and with the linen mitre shall he be attired . . ." (Lev. 16:4). These were made from white flax,

hence their designation "the white garments," and had to be woven with six-ply thread.

The High Priest had two coats which he wore on the Day of Atonement, one for the morning, and the other for the evening. At the conclusion of the Day of Atonement, he would never again wear the white garments in which he had officiated. They were left in the place where he removed them, as the verse indicates: "And Aaron shall come into

The High Priest attired in the mitre and plate.

the tabernacle of the congregation, and he shall put off the linen garments, which he put on when he went into the holy place, and he shall leave them there" (ibid. v. 23).

The ordinary priests wore four garments all year round that were identical with the "white garments" worn by the High Priest on the Day of Atonement: "And for Aaron's sons thou shalt make coats, and thou shalt make for them girdles, and bonnets shalt thou make for them. . . . And

thou shalt make them linen breeches . . ." (Ex. 28:40, 28:42).

Five materials were used to create the priestly garments: (1) gold; (2) *techelet*, sky-blue wool; (3) dark red wool; (4) crimson wool; and (5) twisted linen.

The gold was beaten into thin sheets, and then cut into fine threads. The *techelet* sky-blue color was a dye obtained from an aquatic invertebrate known as *chilazon*. The exact identification of this animal, and the method used to produce the dye, is the subject of extensive research. While various attempts have been made to conclusively identify the *chilazon*, it is believed to be the Mediterranean snail known as *Murex trunculus*.

The dark-red color (said to more closely resemble purple), *argaman* in Hebrew, is also derived from a snail, possibly the *Murex trunculus* as well. According to this theory, the difference in color is a product of the amount of time the substance is initially exposed to sunlight.

The crimson color is produced from a worm referred to in the Bible as the "crimson worm," *tola'at shani*, which has been identified as *Kermes biblicus*, the conchineal insect.

The Hebrew word used here for "linen" is *shesh*, which literally means "six." This indicates that each thread used in these garments is required to be a six-ply linen thread.

Some of the garments were composed of all five ingredients; some contained three or four; some contained only one.

The ephod and breastplate were made of all five materials. "And they shall make the ephod of gold, of blue, and of purple, of scarlet, and fine twined linen, with cunning work" (Ex. 28:26) and "And thou shalt make the breastplate of judgment with cunning work; after the work of the ephod thou shalt make it; of gold, of blue, and of purple, and of scarlet, and of fine twined linen, shalt thou make it" (ibid. v. 15).

Three different girdles were worn by the priests in the Holy Temple: (1) the High Priest's year-round girdle, part of the "golden garments," embroidered with blue, purple and scarlet dyed wools, and twined linen: "And a girdle of fine twined linen, and blue, purple and scarlet, of needlework" (ibid. 39:29); (2) the girdle worn by the High Priest on the Day of Atonement, one of the "white garments," made only of six-ply linen, as the verse states: ". . . and shall be girded with a linen girdle" (Lev. 16:4); and (3) the girdle of the ordinary priests: regarding this item, there are two opinions among scholars. Some maintain that it was the same as the girdle belonging to the set of "golden garments," and thus consisting of four materials; others believe that it belongs to the "white garments" category and was made of linen alone.

The robe was decorated with pomegranates: "And beneath upon the hem of it [the robe] thou shalt make pomegranates of blue, and of purple, and of scarlet . . ." (Ex. 28:33).

The bottom of the robe was also decorated with bells that, like the High Priest's plate, were made of pure gold: "A golden bell and a pomegranate . . . upon the hem of the

Within the Sanctuary. The High Priest, attired in the eight "golden garments," kneels toward the curtain in the direction of the Holy of Holies. To the left of the golden incense altar, a priest adjusts the lights of the menorah; at right, the golden table of the showbread.

robe round about" (ibid. v. 34) and "And thou shalt make a plate of pure gold" (ibid. v. 36).

The robe was made exclusively of blue-dyed wool: "And thou shalt make the robe of the ephod all of blue" (ibid. v. 31). Its threads were 12-ply.

One of the most important of the High Priest's garments was the ephod, a sort of apron worn on top of his other garments at the back while, at the front, it was fastened by a long belt, opposite his heart, that was woven into the entire length of the ephod's upper hem. There were two shoulder straps sewn onto the belt that went behind, up and slightly over the upper corners of the garment, over the priest's shoulders. The settings for the two onyx stones were attached at the ends of these straps, on the shoulders.

The ephod covered the back of the body. Some opinions describe it as a sort of half-cape; others, more like a skirt. It was long, extending from just below the elbows down to the heels and it was slightly wider than a man's back, since it extended a little toward the front on both sides.

An onyx stone was fixed in settings of gold on each of the High Priest's shoulders, and the names of the tribes of Israel were engraved upon them. "And thou shalt take two onyx stones, and grave on them the names of the children of Israel: six of their names on one stone, and the other six names of the rest on the second stone, according to their birth" (Ex. 28:9–10). The Bible calls these two stones "remembrance stones," as it is written, "And thou shalt put the two stones upon the shoulders of the ephod for stones of memorial unto the children of Israel: and Aaron shall bear their names before the Lord upon his two shoulders for a memorial" (ibid. v. 12).

Another two square gold settings were fixed on the High Priest's shoulders, directly under the onyx stones. Golden chains extended from these settings to the golden hooks in the rings of the breastplate, in order to fasten the breastplate to the ephod. "And thou shalt make the breastplate of judgment with cunning work; after the work of the ephod thou shalt make it; of gold, of blue, and of purple, and of scarlet, and of fine twined linen, shalt thou make it" (ibid. v. 15).

This garment was called *choshen mishpat* in Hebrew, which means the "breastplate of *judgment*" or "*decision*." Square-shaped and worn over the heart, it was so called because of the unique role it played in helping to render fateful decisions. It was a patterned brocade like the ephod, woven from gold, blue, purple and scarlet wool, and twined linen. The breastplate was set with four rows of small square stones, in settings of knitted or braided gold and each row contained three stones. These represented the twelve tribes of Israel and the name of the tribe was engraved on each stone.

"And thou shalt set in it settings of stones, even four rows of stones: the first row shall be a *sardius*, a *topaz*, and a *carbuncle*: this shall be the first row. And the second row shall be an *emerald*, a *sapphire*, and a *diamond*. And the third row a *ligure*, an *agate*, and an *amethyst*. And the fourth row a *beryl*, and an *onyx*, and a *jasper*: they shall be set in gold in their inclosings. And the stones shall be with the names of the children of Israel, twelve, according to their names, like the engravings of a signet; every one with his name shall they be according to the twelve tribes" (ibid. v. 17–21).

The translation of the names of these 12 stones is by no means definitive. The exact identification of these stones is

The High Priest wearing the breastplate.

(opposite) An artist's depiction of the breastplate, showing the Hebrew names of the tribes of Israel. Various gems are suggested here as possibilities for the garment's precious stones.

THE BREAST PLATE of the JEWISH HIGH PRIEST.

actually one of the most difficult and elusive of all Temple-related studies. The Hebrew names of these stones are not commonly used, and no description of them appears anywhere in the verses themselves.

Like the two onyx shoulder stones, the Bible states that the purpose of the 12 stones is to be "a memorial before the Lord continually" (Ex. 28:29). When the High Priest bore the breastplate into the holy place, Israel was remembered for peace. The sages taught that the ephod served to invoke the cause of Israel's sustenance and material welfare, and the breastplate her salvation, and deliverance from her enemies.

"And thou shalt put in the breastplate of judgment the Urim and the Thummim; and they shall be upon Aaron's heart, when he goeth in before the Lord" (Ex. 28:30).

The Urim and Thummim were the famed, oracle-like aspect of the breastplate by which a Heavenly answer was received for important questions. According to most authoritative opinions, the expression "Urim and Thummim" actually refers *not* to the breastplate itself but to the mystical Divine name of God, which was written on a piece of parchment and inserted into a flap of the garment. The presence of the name facilitated the reception of Divine guidance through the shining of specific letters on the stones.

At the time the tabernacle was erected in the desert, Moses took the original Urim and Thummim and placed it inside the breastplate of judgment, after Aaron had donned the ephod: ". . . and put the ephod upon him, and he girded him with the curious girdle of the ephod . . . and he put the breastplate upon him; also he put in the breastplate the Urim and the Thummim" (Lev. 8:7–8).

The process of asking for Divine aid through the "Urim and Thummim" was done in the following manner. When a question arose whose implications were so consequential that the entire congregation of Israel would be affected—such as, for example, the question of whether or not to go to war—then, the king of Israel (or the commanding army officer) would ask his question before the High Priest.

The High Priest stood facing the ark of the testimony, and the questioner stood behind him, facing the priest's back. The questioner did not speak aloud but posed his query quietly, to himself, like someone who prays in silence before his Creator. The High Priest, enveloped by the spirit of Divine inspiration, gazed at the breastplate and, by meditating upon the holy names of God, was able to receive the answer through a prophetic vision—the letters on the stones of the breastplate, which would shine forth *in his eyes* in a special manner, would spell out the answer to the question.

Josephus Flavius writes that the stones also shone brilliantly when Israel went forth into battle. This was considered as an auspicious sign for their victory (*Antiquities* 3.8.9).

The High Priest and the King of Israel posing a question to the "Urim and Thummim" in the Holy of Holies. One way in which the Holy One chose to manifest Himself to Israel throughout the generations was through the Urim and Thummim in the Holy Temple. Whenever a question of great national import arose in Israel, the Urim and Thummim was consulted.

According to most scholars, the robe was seamlessly woven from one piece of fabric, and slipped on over the head. It was worn over the tunic, which was longer by one handbreadth, so it was visible underneath the robe. The neck was round, with a doubled hem that was woven and not sewn. The garment extended all the way down to the priest's feet. There is a difference of opinion as to whether it had sleeves.

The hem of the robe was woven over doubly in order to prevent it from ripping due to the weight of the pomegranates and bells but again, it was not sewn: "And

there shall be an hole in the top of it, in the midst thereof: it shall have a binding of woven work round about the hole of it, as it were the hole of an habergeon, that it be not rent" (Ex. 28:32). These pomegranates were actually hollow spheres of fabric shaped like the fruit.

The crown was a thin plate constructed of one piece of pure, solid gold but, unlike the royal crowns which are worn on top of the head, this was worn across the forehead and extended from ear to ear.

This crown was inscribed with the words "Holiness to

(above left) The crown of the High Priest, one of his four "golden garments." It was made of pure gold, and worn across his forehead.

(above right) The High Priest attired in his eight "golden garments."

the Lord." At the time of the destruction of Herod's Temple, this was written in one line, according to the eye-witness testimony of Rabbi Eliezer, the son of Rabbi Yose, who saw the crown in Rome (both the Talmud and Josephus inform us that after the destruction of the Second Temple, many of the sacred vessels were plundered and taken to Rome, where they were publicly displayed for many years).

"And it shall be upon Aaron's forehead, that Aaron may bear the iniquity of the holy things [specifically, this is a reference to ritual impurity], which the children of Israel

shall hallow in all their holy gifts; and it shall be always upon his forehead, that they may be accepted before the Lord" (Ex. 28:38).

The crown had three small holes: two at each end, and one in the center, along the upper edge. Running through these holes were blue-dyed threads, the ends of which were fastened at the back of the priest's head.

The turban was placed on the priest's head in such a way that a space was left between it and the plate upon his forehead. This space enabled the High Priest to wear the *tefillin*, the phylacteries of the head (see Deut. 6:8). The middle blue thread was extended over the turban, where it was tied to the other strands at the back of his head: "And thou shalt put it on a blue lace, that it may be upon the mitre; upon the forefront of the mitre it shall be" (Ex. 28:37).

"And they made coats of fine linen of woven work for Aaron, and for his sons" (Ex. 39:27). The coat clung close to the body and extended from the priest's neck, down to the feet, just above the heels. As it was one piece, it was donned by placing it over the head.

The Bible describes "a broidered coat" (ibid. 28:4). This indicates that the coat was not woven with an ordinary cross-weave pattern but of a pattern consisting of many small boxes, or cells.

"And thou shalt . . . make the mitre of fine linen. . . . And for Aaron's sons . . . and bonnets shalt thou make for them" (Ex. 28:39–40). The High Priest's mitre was made of a narrow strip of white linen, measuring 16 cubits (approximately 24 feet). It was wound around the top of the priest's head after the manner in which one dresses a wound, wrapping the material over and over. Josephus maintains that a cap of sky-blue wool was placed over the High Priest's white linen turban. Over this cap, he continues, three horizontal gold bands were placed, topped off with a floral decoration. Thus the turban appeared like a crown, with an opening in front to allow for the placement of the *tefillin* and "crown"—the gold plate on his forehead.

Many authorities hold that the ordinary priests' hat was exactly the same as that of the High Priest, except that the former's was wound on, and the latter's was simply placed on. Others maintain that the High Priest's is correctly called a turban because of its shape, whereas the hat of the ordinary priests was also wound around, but it had a conical shape upon the head.

The belt of white linen was only "three fingerbreadths" (2 1/4 inches) wide, records both the Talmud and Maimonides, but it was made from an exceedingly long piece of fabric.

Josephus describes the belt as being hollow like the skin shed by a snake (*Antiquities* 3.7.2) and was a work of "embroidery." When used in this context of Temple furnishings, the Bible uses this term to indicate that the

The High Priest sprinkling from the blood of the bullock, once facing upward, and seven times facing down. This is not done on the curtain itself, but opposite the curtain and the place of the ark, indicated by the protrusion of the two poles through the curtain.

same design was featured on both sides of the material. Although the belt itself was made of linen, the embroidery—a floral design—was done with three colored wool threads, and attached to the white linen background. This combination of wool and linen together in garments is normally forbidden (see Lev. 19:19), but it was permitted for the priestly garments.

The belt was wrapped many times around the body. Its purpose was to separate the upper and lower portions of the body, for Jewish law obligates this separation during prayer or the mention of anything holy. Josephus states that when worn, the two ends of the belt hung in front, down to the priest's ankles (*Antiquities* 3.7.2). However, during the actual service the priest would cast these two ends over his left shoulder, to prevent them from interfering with his work.

"And thou shalt make them linen breeches to cover their nakedness; from the loins even unto the thighs they shall reach" (Ex. 28:42). This verse indicates that the priest's breeches did not serve the same purpose as the other sacred garments which were "for honor and for beauty," glorifying the sacred office and having a deeper significance, such as the power to atone. This does not apply to the breeches, however, whose function was one of modesty alone.

These breeches were closed, without the usual openings, and they extended from the waist down to the knees. According to most authorities, the upper hem was hollow and had a lace running through it, which was tied at the waist. Josephus, however, maintains that these laces were around the knees (*Antiquities* 3.7.1).

"There were seven gates in the courtyard: three in the north, three in the south, and one in the east . . . the one in the east is the Nikanor Gate, and within it were two chambers, one on the right side and one on the left. One was the Chamber of Phineas the Wardrober, and the other was a chamber where the High Priest's meal offering was prepared" (*Midot* 1,4). During the time of the Second Temple, Phineas the Wardrober was the official who supervised the uniforms and the dressing of the priests.

When it came time to put on the vestments of their office, the ordinary priests donned the breeches without removing their own personal clothes which, afterwards, were removed from underneath. Then the coat was put on, and the belt was tied. The hat was put on last.

The High Priest dressed in the same manner. After the belt was tied, the High Priest put on the blue robe, the ephod was placed over the robe and the breastplate was fastened to the ephod. When these garments were in place, the High Priest's head was wrapped in the turban, and then the crown was tied on his forehead.

The priests wore no shoes or sandals; they would walk barefoot on the marble floors of the Temple courts. This was done to preserve the sanctity not only of the Temple itself but of the Temple complex.

The Day of Atonement

Unlike other ceremonies throughout the year, all of the sacred tasks performed on Yom Kippur, the Day of Atonement, had to be carried out by the High Priest himself. He alone was responsible for every aspect of the Divine service on this most holy and awesome day, which included 15 separate sacrifices as well as the menorah, incense and other services.

There was much to be done in order to prepare the High Priest for this momentous day. Just as Aaron, the first High Priest, isolated himself ("And ye shall not go out of the door of the tabernacle of the congregation in seven days, until the days of your consecration be at an end: for seven days shall he consecrate you" [Lev. 8:33]), so too the High Priest left his own home and family a full week before the advent of Yom Kippur, and withdrew to his chamber in the Holy Temple. Another priest was designated as the High Priest's replacement in case he inadvertently became defiled and could not purify himself in time to conduct the service. An extra set of the High Priest's "golden garments" was prepared accordingly for this potential substitute.

Throughout the week, the High Priest diligently studied the laws relating to the tasks which he had to perform on the sacred day, and he would also conduct certain aspects of the daily service himself (even though it was not his exclusive duty) in order to familiarize himself with them. For example, during these days he himself would sprinkle the blood of the daily sacrifice onto the altar in the morning and in the evening; he would offer up the incense on the golden incense altar; and he would attend to the service of the menorah (cleaning the used oil and wicks, adjusting new wicks and adding the proper measure of oil to each flame).

This was a period of intense preparation and review. Each day, the elders of the Sanhedrin (the supreme rabbinical court) would read to him from the biblical portion that relates to the service.

On the morning preceding the Day of Atonement, the High Priest stood in the Eastern Gate as the cows, rams and sheep were marched before him, scrutinizing them intently while reviewing in his mind all of the precepts he had studied regarding the order of their sacrifice, as well as other aspects of the service he would be conducting the following day.

On the Day of Atonement itself, no one was permitted to witness the High Priest actually performing the incense service for the Bible specifically states: "And there shall be no man in the tabernacle of the congregation when he goeth in to make an atonement in the holy place, until he come out . . ." (Lev.16:17).

On the night which begins the Day of Atonement itself, the High Priest was forbidden to sleep in case he inadvertently became defiled while sleeping and was thereby rendered impure. Should such a mishap befall him, he would be unfit to conduct the service in the morning. He would stay awake the entire night and

The High Priest standing at the Eastern Gate on the morning before the Day of Atonement, as cows, rams and sheep are marched before him.

expound upon the Bible, explaining many verses according to homiletic interpretations, or others would read to him from the Books of Job, Ezra, and Chronicles. Various commentators have expressed a number of engaging opinions as to why it was these three specific books that were read aloud before the High Priest. Some point out that their content is particularly interesting, thus preventing the listener from becoming drowsy.

Whenever the High Priest felt that sleep was beginning to overcome him, the young priests-in-training would snap their fingers and declare, "Master! High Priest! Rise up,

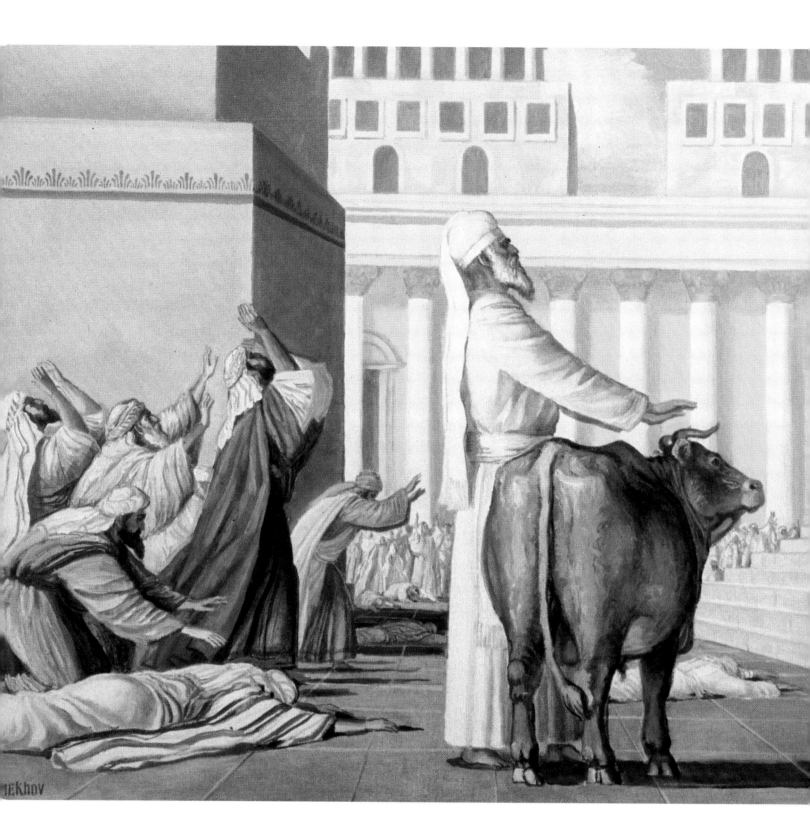

and stand upon the floor!'' The priests served barefoot in the Temple and standing on the cold marble floor for a moment would drive away the desire for sleep.

"And the Lord spake unto Moses after the death of the two sons of Aaron, when they offered before the Lord, and died; and the Lord said unto Moses, Speak unto Aaron thy brother, that he come not at all times into the holy place within the vail before the mercy seat, which is upon the ark; that he die not: for I will appear in the cloud upon the mercy seat.

"Thus shall Aaron come into the holy place: with a young bullock for a sin offering, and a ram for a burnt offering. He shall put on the holy linen coat, and he shall have the linen breeches upon his flesh, and shall be girded with a linen girdle, and with the linen mitre shall he be attired: these are holy garments; therefore shall he wash his flesh in water, and so put them on. And he shall take of the congregation of the children of Israel two kids of the goats for a sin offering, and one ram for a burnt offering. And Aaron shall offer his bullock of the sin offering, which is for himself, and he make an atonement for himself, and for his house'' (Lev. 16:1–6).

The bullock that the High Priest sacrificed as his own personal act of atonement (and for his family as well) had to be his personal property, ''. . . the sin offering, which is for himself.''

The High Priest drew near to the animal. Facing the Sanctuary, he placed his two hands on the bullock's head, between its horns, and made his confession:

I beseech You, O Lord;
I have sinned, rebelled, and transgressed against You,
I, and my household;
I beseech You, O Lord,
Grant atonement for the sins,
and for the iniquities and transgressions
which I have committed against You,
I, and my household.
As it is written in the Torah
of Your servant, Moses:
For on this day
atonement shall be made for you,
to purify you from all your sins
—before the Lord you shall be purified.

(above left) The High Priest confessing over the bullock as the priests and congregation prostrate themselves upon hearing the Sacred Name.

(above right) The High Priest ascending the spiral staircase to his immersion chamber. Another priest follows, carrying the white garments for his change of clothing.

The High Priest casting lots (detail above) over two goats on the Day of Atonement, to determine which would be the scapegoat and which would be the sacrifice.

During the prayers on this awesome day, the High Priest would utter the Ineffable Name of God known as the Tetragrammaton, which was made up of four letters that are transliterated as YHWH. In Hebrew, this is known as God's "proper name" (*Shem HaMeforash*) and denotes the Holy One as the ultimate source of all existence. Usually, this most holy name was not pronounced as it was written, and was not used at all outside of the Holy Temple—where it was used rarely. During the course of the services on the Day of Atonement, however, the High Priest would have occasion to utter it ten times.

Three of these would be during his confession and, when the congregation assembled in the court heard the holy name of God from the lips of the High Priest, they responded, "Blessed be the Name of His glorious kingdom, for ever and ever." This was based on the verse in the song of Moses: "Because I will publish the name of the Lord: ascribe ye greatness unto our God" (Deut. 32:3).

All the Day of Atonement service was frought with poignancy, tense anticipation and deep personal stirrings of repentance, yet one of the most dramatic moments of the day was the lottery conducted by the High Priest to choose the scapegoat, which was to be cast off as an atonement for Israel's sins.

After making his confession over the bullock, the High Priest would walk to the eastern section of the court, facing the entrance, accompanied by two men: at his right, the "assistant," the priest who was designated as a stand-in should the High Priest be rendered unfit and, at his left, the head of the family clan who was responsible for the service in the Temple on that day of the week.

In the eastern sector of the court, to the north of the altar, two goats were placed in preparation for the lottery: "And he shall take of the congregation of the children of Israel two kids of the goats for a sin offering, and one ram for a burnt offering. . . . And he shall take the two goats, and present them before the Lord at the door of the tabernacle of the congregation. And Aaron shall cast lots upon the two goats; one lot for the Lord, and the other lot for the scapegoat [Hebrew, *azazel*]" (Lev. 16:5–8).

In the wooden lottery box that was kept there were the two lots. On one lot the two Hebrew words meaning "for the Lord" were written, while the other was inscribed with

khov

the Hebrew word "for *azazel*." *Azazel* is actually the name of the place to which the scapegoat was sent, a high, rocky precipice in the Judean desert from which the goat was cast to its death.

Originally, the lots were made of wood, probably boxwood, but during the term of office of the High Priest Yehoshua ben Gamla, they were prepared from gold, to increase the honor of the holy day.

Flanked by the two men, the High Priest thrust his hands into the lottery box and stirred the two lots within in order to ascertain that he had no notion which was inscribed "For the Lord." It was considered an auspicious sign from Heaven if that lot were to be drawn by his right hand.

The High Priest then placed these lots upon the heads of the goats between their horns. That which he raised up in his right hand was placed upon the animal to his right, the other upon the animal to his left. When placing the lot of "For the Lord" upon the sacrifice, he recited aloud the words "For the Lord, a sin offering," once again pronouncing the holy Ineffable Name of God, while all the priests and Israelites present repeated the verse "Blessed be the Name . . ."

The High Priest then tied a length of crimson-dyed wool between the horns of the scapegoat, and tied a similar length of wool around the neck of the goat which was to be sacrificed. The wool was dyed crimson in accordance with the verse, ". . . though your sins be as scarlet, they shall be as white as snow; though they be red like crimson, they

The High Priest placing his hands upon the bullock's head as he confesses, based on the verse "And Aaron shall lay both his hands . . ." (Lev. 16:21).

shall be as wool" (Isa. 1:18).

Having prepared the two goats, the High Priest left them and proceeded with other aspects of this singular day's ceremonies. He would return to the sacrifice and the scapegoat only later, after the services of the bullock and the incense were completed. All the various components and aspects of the Yom Kippur service had to be done according to a specific order.

Now the High Priest once again approached his own offering, the bullock. He again confessed over the animal, but this time he confessed on behalf of all his fellow priests. Once again he placed his hands on the animal's head, between its horns, and pronouncing the Ineffable Name he recited his plea:

(above) The mizrak *(containment vessel) used to gather the blood from the sacrifices to be brought to the altar.*

(right) The High Priest using a mizrak *vessel to sprinkle the sacrificial blood.*

(opposite page) Silver shovel used for the removal of ashes.

I beseech You, O Lord;
I have sinned, rebelled, and transgressed against You,
I and my household,
And the sons of Aaron, Your holy people;
I beseech You, O Lord,
Grant atonement for the sins,
and for the iniquities and transgressions
which I have committed against You,
I and my household,
And the sons of Aaron Your holy people—.
As it is written in the Torah
of Your servant, Moses:
For on this day
atonement shall be made for you,
to purify you from all your sins
—before the Lord you shall be purified.

Again, the congregation responded with the words "Blessed be the Name of His glorious kingdom, for ever and ever."

At the conclusion of his second confession, the High Priest slaughtered the bullock, receiving the offering's blood in the *mizrak* vessel which he then gave to another priest. The High Priest immediately went to prepare for the incense service, while the other priest stood outside the entrance to the Sanctuary and held this vessel, continuously moving it with a stirring motion. This was done in order to prevent its contents from beginning to congeal, since this would invalidate it from being dashed upon the altar.

Thus occupied with the *mizrak*, the priest waited for the return of the High Priest, who would take the *mizrak* into the Sanctuary. In the meantime, the High Priest ascended to the top of the altar in the court, carrying a golden incense shovel with a specially long handle—designed to aid him in performing the particularly difficult movements required to conduct the incense service alone on this holy day. The High Priest stirred the fire with the incense shovel and he gathered some of the burning coals from the midst of the fire in it. After descending the ramp, he returned to where the priest waited with the *mizrak*, and placed the incense shovel and its coals on the floor, next to him.

"And he shall take a censer full of burning coals of fire from off the altar before the Lord, and his hands full of sweet incense beaten small, and bring it within the vail" (Lev. 16:12).

After he had placed the shovelful of burning coals on the floor near the Sanctuary, other priests now brought the two other items the High Priest would use to conduct the incense service: a large golden spoon, rather like a small cup with a long handle, which was brought from the Chamber of Vessels; and a golden shovel, filled with finely ground incense, which was brought from the Chamber of the Avtinas family where the incense was prepared.

The High Priest would then place the incense into the golden spoon, holding it with his left hand and using his right to pick up the censer full of burning coals from the floor before him. In this manner, carrying the spoonful of incense and the shovel of coals, he entered the Sanctuary up to the two curtains which separated the Holy (the Sanctuary, which housed the menorah, table and incense altar) from the Holy of Holies.

In the First Temple, a wall the thickness of one *amah* (approximately 48–60 centimeters) divided these two areas. However, in the Second Temple two curtains once again separated them, as in the days of the tabernacle. The

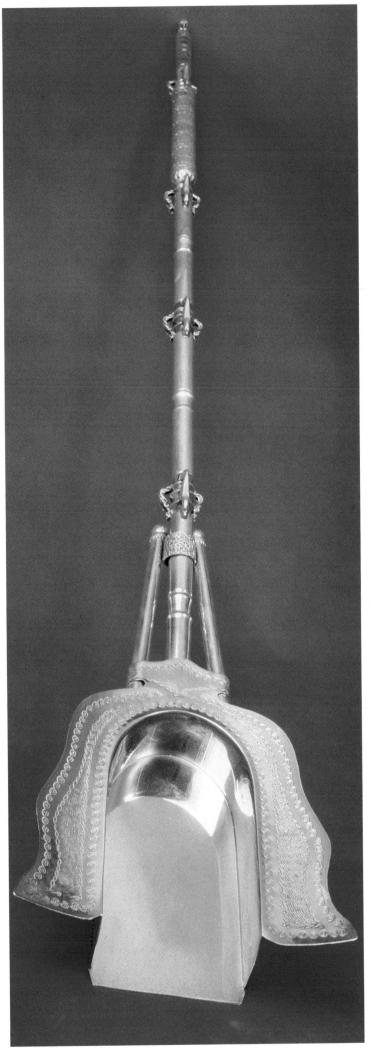

distance between the curtains was one *amah*, like that wall which stood in Solomon's Temple.

One end of each of these two curtains was folded over on the outside and pinned up by a golden clasp, the outer on the southern side, and the inner, on the northern side. Thus an aisle was formed between the two curtains and the High Priest, carrying the golden spoon and the shovel, walked between them until he reached the northern side of the inner curtain—the spot where it was held up.

Here he stood at the opening of the Holy of Holies before turning and facing south with the length of curtain to his left so that he could walk to the center of the room to stand in the place known as "between the poles"— between the two poles of the Ark of the Covenant. However, in the days of the Second Temple, the Holy of Holies was empty.

The Ark of the Covenant was a box constructed of acacia wood, and its exact dimensions are listed in chapter 25 of the Book of Exodus as 2 1/2 cubits long, 1 1/2 cubits wide, and 1 1/2 cubits high. It was covered, and lined within, with pure gold, and a gold rim ran all along its top.

Four rings were placed on the four corners of the ark,

two on each side. Into these rings, two carrying poles of gold-covered acacia wood were placed. A golden cover was placed on the ark, with a golden cherub hammered out from each of the two ends. These had winged bodies and faces like human infants—one male and the other female. The two cherubs faced each other and their wings spread upward and thus shielded the cover.

The "testimony," the Tablets of the Law which Moses brought down from Mount Sinai, were placed inside the ark, and throughout the era of the desert tabernacle and the days of the First Temple, this was housed in the Holy of Holies, which was entered only by the High Priest and then only on the Day of Atonement.

The Holy of Holies is where the *Shechina*, the Divine Presence, rested: "And there I will meet with thee, and I will commune with thee from above the mercy seat, from between the two cherubims which are upon the ark of the testimony . . ." (Ex. 25:22).

Within the Holy of Holies on Mount Moriah was the "Foundation Stone." This jutted up the width of three fingerbreadths above the ground and when the ark was

The Ark of the Covenant, constructed of pure gold, contained the original Tablets of the Law which Moses received from God at the revelation on Mount Sinai.

housed in the Holy of Holies, it rested on top of this stone. The presence of the Foundation Stone had been revealed in the days of King David and the prophet Samuel. It was called "foundation" because, according to tradition, it predated time and was the very foundation upon which God created the world.

When the tabernacle and the First Temple stood, the High Priest faced the holy Ark of the Covenant and put the shovel of coals down, directly between its two poles. In the Second Temple era, however, he would put the shovel down on the Foundation Stone itself, in the place where the poles would be extending had the ark been there.

Once the High Priest had put down the shovel, he had to take the fine incense powder from the spoon into his hands—for when he placed the incense on the coals, it had to be directly from his palms, the "double handful."

The High Priest then placed the incense onto the coals in the shovel, on the side of the shovel away from where he stood, so that he would not be burned as the flames ignited. He then waited momentarily, until the entire chamber was filled with smoke.

(opposite) The tabernacle and the Israelite camp at the foot of Mount Sinai, depicted here with the "cloud of glory" covering its top, representing the Shechina, *the Divine Presence of God. The Israelites encamped around the mountain according to their tribes.*

(opposite page) Booths, or way stations, ten in all, set up along the route from Jerusalem to the cliff in the wilderness, where the scapegoat met its end.

The High Priest spilling the blood on the golden altar. Holding the containment vessel, he would sprinkle once with his finger from the sacrificial blood along the horns of the altar and afterwards, seven times upon the altar itself.

The Yom Kippur incense offering completed, he then left the Holy of Holies with extreme reverence, through the two curtains back into the Sanctuary without once having turned his back on the holy place.

In the next stage of the Yom Kippur service, the High Priest returned to the priest who had been waiting for him outside the entrance since the bullock was slaughtered, holding the *mizrak* and moving it about so that the blood would not congeal. The High Priest now took this vessel from his colleague and returned to the Holy of Holies a second time. Walking between the two curtains and carrying the vessel holding the blood of his offering, he came back to the spot "between the poles" where he placed the incense on the coals atop the Foundation Stone.

There, as commanded in the Book of Leviticus (16:14), he took some of the bullock's blood, and with his forefinger he sprinkled it above the east side of the ark cover. He then sprinkled with his forefinger seven times directly toward the ark cover. Afterwards he left the Holy of Holies, again without turning his back on it, and placed the vessel on a golden stand within the Sanctuary.

In the court outside, the goat which had been designated as "For the Lord" by the lottery was now brought to the High Priest who slaughtered the animal and gathered its blood into another *mizrak* vessel. He then entered the Holy of Holies a third time, carrying the vessel containing the blood of the goat. He entered the chamber exactly as he did the previous times, and again walked to the same precise spot. Here, "between the poles," he sprinkled the blood as before and then left, placing this vessel on a second golden stand pre-positioned within the Sanctuary.

He did not leave the Sanctuary but took the first *mizrak*, containing the blood of the bullock, from the first stand where he had originally placed it. Facing the curtains that separated the Holy from the Holy of Holies, he stood opposite the place that he had entered unto three times— "between the poles" of the ark. This time, he dashed the blood of the bullock *outside the curtain* but toward the same spot, in the same manner we have described. Next, he placed this *mizrak* down on its stand, once again took the second vessel containing the blood of the sacrificial goat, and repeated his action against the curtain.

Finally, while still in the Sanctuary, the High Priest mixed the contents of both vessels together. He poured the *mizrak* containing the bullock's blood into that of the goat, and then poured the mixed contents of this full vessel back into the empty one so that they blended completely, as described in the Book of Leviticus (16:18): "And he shall go out unto the altar that is before the Lord, and make an atonement for it; and shall *take of the blood of the bullock, and of the blood of the goat*, and put it upon the horns of the altar round about." We shall now look at the portion of the service referred to by this verse.

Having completed the sprinkling inside the Holy of Holies and within the Sanctuary, the Bible instructed him to sprinkle on the corners of "the altar that is before the Lord." This expression refers only to the golden incense altar within the Sanctuary; the outer altar that stands in the court is never referred to as being "before the Lord." As to the Bible's instructions that he is now to "go out," this indicates that he is to go out from the place where he had been standing by the curtain, and serve on the outer side of the altar. The High Priest walked around the incense altar and sprinkled blood on each of its four corners. Afterwards, he cleared away some of the coals on top and

exposed some of the gold surface of the altar. On this area, the "floor" of the small incense altar, he sprinkled an additional seven times, according to the verse: "And he shall sprinkle of the blood upon it with his finger seven times . . ." (ibid. v. 19). Whatever was left in the *mizrak*, he poured out onto the western side of the outer altar's foundation, in keeping with the instruction: ". . . and shall pour all the blood of the bullock at the bottom of the altar of the burnt offering, which is at the door of the tabernacle of the congregation" (Lev. 4:7).

The High Priest now returned to the place where the scapegoat was waiting, opposite the Eastern Gate through which it would be led off into the desert.

Placing his two hands on the animal's head between its horns, the High Priest now offered his confession for the entire nation of Israel: "And when he hath made an end of reconciling the holy place, and the tabernacle of the

congregation, and the altar, he shall bring the live goat: And Aaron shall lay both his hands upon the head of the live goat, and confess over him all the iniquities of the children of Israel, and all their transgressions in all their sins, putting them upon the head of the goat . . ." (Lev. 16:20–21).

I beseech You, O Lord;
Grant atonement for the sins,
and for the iniquities and transgressions
which the entire house of Israel
has committed against You,
As it is written in the Torah
of Your servant, Moses:
For on this day
atonement shall be made for you,
to purify you from all your sins
—before the Lord you shall be purified.

The High Priest reading from the Torah scroll once the scapegoat had reached the desert. He stands at the top of the 15 steps leading from the Women's Court to the Court of Israel, while those assembled below read along from their own Torah scrolls.

The congregation responded with the words "Blessed be the Name of His glorious kingdom, for ever and ever."

After confessing for the children of Israel, the High Priest handed the scapegoat to the individual who had been designated to lead it into the desert. This, too, was considered a great privilege. Even though it was not an intrinsic part of the service and therefore could even be done by an Israelite, it was a privilege that was usually jealously guarded by the priests.

A special bridge connected the Temple Mount complex with the Mount of Anointment, and the scapegoat was led over this bridge to the outskirts of the city and then into the desert. All along the way between Jerusalem and the cliff that was the scapegoat's destination, a series of way stations had been manned since before the onset of Yom Kippur to ensure that the mission was successfully completed. Men had been pre-positioned at equidistant locations to render the scapegoat's warden any assistance that he might require, and to accompany him along the way.

These "stations" were actually booths where food and drink were kept for the priest leading the scapegoat should he feel physically unable to continue without breaking his fast. A number of distinguished citizens of Jerusalem accompanied the priest as far as the first booth; from there, men from each booth accompanied him as far as the next station.

Arriving at the cliff, the priest removed the crimson wool that the High Priest had tied to the scapegoat's horns. He divided it into two pieces, tying one to the animal's horns and the second to a rock so that he would be able to see when the crimson color had turned white and know that atonement had been made for Israel's sins. Then he pushed the goat backward with his two hands.

After he had accomplished his task, the priest who had led the scapegoat walked back to the last booth, and waited there until dark before he returned to Jerusalem—for he had only been permitted to travel this distance in order to fulfill the duty of the scapegoat. After having given the scapegoat to his colleague, the High Priest had to wait until he received word that the scapegoat had reached the desert, and thus he could proceed to the next stage of the day's service. In addition to the crimson wool on the Sanctuary miraculously turning white, this information reached the Temple another way. Scouts were positioned at high points all along the route to the cliff and, as the goat was led from one station to the next, these scouts would signal to each other by waving cloths and, when the scapegoat had finally been cast off, the news was relayed back to the Temple through their scouts' signals.

On receiving this news, the High Priest descended to the Women's Court and read aloud from the Book of Leviticus (chapter 16, the reading for Yom Kippur) before the congregation.

At the end of this awesome day, when the service had been concluded, the entire multitude of worshippers accompanied the High Priest back to his own home.

The Festival of Sukkot (Tabernacles)

Each of the three major festivals has a traditional designation. Passover, commemorating the Exodus from Egypt, is known as "the time of our freedom." Shavuot is "the time of the giving of our Torah" and Sukkot (The Festival of Tabernacles) is "the time of our joy." These three holidays were the occasion of pilgrimage up to Jerusalem and the Holy Temple.

"And the Lord spake unto Moses, saying, Speak unto the children of Israel, saying, The fifteenth day of this seventh month shall be the feast of tabernacles for seven days unto the Lord. . . . Seven days ye shall offer an offering made by fire unto the Lord . . .

"And ye shall take you on the first day the boughs of goodly trees, branches of palm trees, and the boughs of thick trees, and willows of the brook; and ye shall rejoice before the Lord your God seven days. And ye shall keep it a feast unto the Lord seven days in the year. It shall be a statute for ever in your generations: ye shall celebrate it in the seventh month.

"Ye shall dwell in booths seven days; all that are Israelites born shall dwell in booths. That your generations may know that I made the children of Israel to dwell in booths, when I brought them out of the land of Egypt: I am the Lord your God." (Lev. 23:33–43).

The rejoicing was felt most strongly in the Holy Temple, the focal point of Jewish worship. In addition to the biblical commandment of rejoicing with "the four species" (the *etrog*, *lulav*, myrtle, and willow) on Sukkot, two other commandments were observed in the Holy Temple. However, these two practices are not mandated by a verse in the Scriptures; they are included in that body of custom called *halacha le moshe mi-sinai*—details of religious observance that God taught to Moses at Mount Sinai. These were subsequently related by Moses to Joshua, and on to the elders of Israel, and likewise throughout all the generations they were transmitted orally. These two items are the "special commandment of the willow," and the water libation.

The worshippers would place exceptionally long willow branches from Motza, on the outskirts of Jerusalem, all along the foundation of the altar, with their heads bent over the top (opposite). The bringing of these branches each day and their arrangement along the altar was accompanied by trumpet blasts and the sounding of the *shofar* by the priests and Levites. The priests would circle the altar

once, holding their *lulavim* and appealing to the Almighty: "We beseech You, O Lord, please save us! We beseech You, O Lord, please grant us success!" On the seventh, and last, day of the festival, they would circle the altar seven times—as a remembrance of the conquest of Jericho.

Rabbi Meir said, "The people of Jerusalem used to bind their lulavim *with bands of gold" (Sukkah 3,8).*

The other non-biblical commandment observed in the Temple during Sukkot was the water libation. Each morning, during the daily sacrifice, water was poured onto the altar in a special manner in a joyous service conducted with great public ceremony.

At the foot of Mount Moriah, in the City of David, there is a natural spring called Siloam, the source of Jerusalem's water. As it is located literally in the shadow of the Holy Temple, it has always had spiritual significance for Israel.

Each day of the festival, the priests went down to Siloam, accompanied by all the congregation assembled in the Temple. There, they filled a golden flask with 3 *lug* (about 1/2 liter) of the pure water and returned to the Temple through the Water Gate, on the southern side of the court. As they entered the gate, their steps were greeted by the sound of trumpets and *shofar* blasts, in fulfillment of the prophet's words: "Therefore with joy shall ye draw water out of the wells of salvation" (Isa. 12:3).

Once in the Temple, the priest who had the honor of performing this service carried the golden flask up the altar ramp. At the top, he turned to his left, facing the southwest corner where the libations were poured. Two silver cups were fixed on the top of the altar. The one to the east was for the wine libations that were poured during the daily *tamid* sacrifice; the other was designated for this service, which took place exclusively on Sukkot.

Each of these cups had a narrow opening into which the libations were poured. That which received the water libation had a bigger opening than that of the wine, because both were poured at the same time, and they had to reach the bottom of the altar simultaneously.

While the actual act of pouring the water on the altar took place early in the morning, this libation was preceded

Pilgrims making their way to Jerusalem to celebrate the festival of Sukkot in the Holy Temple.

(opposite page) To the sound of trumpet blasts, a priest lowers the golden vessel into the Siloam spring as his colleagues and other celebrants look on. The water will be brought up to the Holy Temple, where it will be poured upon the altar for the water libation.

by celebrations throughout each night of Sukkot. Most of the daily festivities took place in the Women's Court. At the conclusion of the first day of the festival, the priests and Levites prepared this area by erecting raised balconies all along the periphery of the court. Huge lamps were erected in the Women's Court to illuminate the festival of the water libation, each consisting of four containers of oil mounted on a huge pole.

The actual participants in the celebrations were not the common folk, but the greatest scholars and the most pious men of the generation—the heads of the Sanhedrin, the sages, the academy heads and the elders. In the presence of all those assembled in the Holy Temple, these exceedingly righteous men would dance, sing and rejoice. While these

The pilgrimage to Jerusalem evoked an overwhelming feeling of joy in the hearts of the participants, and served to unify the entire nation.

The Temple at dawn.

celebrations were in progress down on the floor of the Women's Court, the Levites stood upon the 15 steps that led up from the court to the Court of Israel, which corresponded to the 15 "steps," the "songs of ascent" mentioned in the Book of Psalms (ch. 120–134). Normally, the Levite choir stood within the Court of Israel, opposite the outer altar and facing the entrance to the Sanctuary. A special platform was located there, just within the Nikanor Gates, and the Levites stood there and sang every day during the daily sacrifices. At the water libation, however, it was upon these steps that they sang and played on their harps, lyres, cymbals and trumpets.

In addition, two priests with silver trumpets stood at either side of the entrance to the great Nikanor Gates. At

dawn's first light, they blew the trumpets to signal that the time had arrived for all to descend to the Siloam spring, to bring up water for the libation. As they began the descent, the entire assemblage began to move out of the court to leave the Temple. The two priests blew the trumpets for the second time when they reached the tenth step, and again when they reached the floor of the Women's Court. They blew longer blasts as they continued to walk, until they reached the Eastern Gate, the gate which led from the Women's Court, out of the Holy Temple complex and onto the Temple Mount. There at the Eastern Gate, the entire congregation turned their backs as one, and stood facing west, in the direction of the court and the Sanctuary.

Now, as the first rays of the dawn began to shine, they gazed upon the Holy Temple, and recited together: "Our fathers stood in this place with their backs toward the Sanctuary of God, and their faces toward the east. They prostrated themselves to the sun in the east. But we—we are to God, and to God our eyes turn. We bow to God and our eyes look to Him in hope." This was a reference to the close of the First Temple era, pharaphrasing the prophet Ezekiel: "And he brought me into the inner court of the Lord's house, and, behold, at the door of the temple of the Lord, between the porch and the altar, were about five and twenty men, with their backs toward the temple of the Lord, and their faces toward the east; and they worshipped the sun toward the east" (Ezek. 8:16).

The Festival of Passover: "Time of Our Freedom"

"And the Lord spake unto Moses and Aaron in the land of Egypt, saying, This month shall be unto you the beginning of months: it shall be the first month of the year to you. . . . And they shall eat the flesh in that night, roast with fire, and unleavened bread; and with bitter herbs they shall eat it. . . . And this day shall be unto you for a memorial; and ye shall keep it a feast to the Lord throughout your generations; ye shall keep it a feast by an ordinance for ever. Seven days shall ye eat unleavened bread. . . . And ye shall observe this thing for an ordinance to thee and to thy sons for ever. And it shall come to pass, when ye come to the land which the Lord will give you, according as he hath promised, that ye shall keep this service. And it shall come to pass, when your children shall say unto you, What mean ye by this service? That ye shall say, It is the sacrifice of the Lord's passover, who passed over the houses of the children of Israel in Egypt, when he smote the Egyptians, and delivered our houses" (Ex. 12:1–27).

"These are the feasts of the Lord, even holy convocations, which ye shall proclaim in their seasons. In the fourteenth day of the first month at even is the Lord's passover. And on the fifteenth day of the same month is the feast of unleavened bread unto the Lord: seven days ye must eat unleavened bread. . . . But ye shall offer an offering made by fire unto the Lord seven days . . ." (Lev. 23:4–8).

The entire Jewish people converged on Jerusalem from the four corners of the ancient world to celebrate Passover in the Holy City. Those who lived nearby had a comparatively easy journey but others came from neighboring lands and some traveled great distances, even from as far away as Rome. The pilgrims came in caravans, numbering hundreds and sometimes even thousands, and each group brought the obligatory "half-shekel" donation to the Temple treasury on behalf of their community.

In Jerusalem, preparations for the influx of such large numbers began early. After the rainy winter, it was important to make sure that the roads were not washed out, and all the approaches to Jerusalem were traversable. The city squares and public areas along the way were also cleared, so that they could function as way stations where the pilgrims might spend the night and replenish their supplies.

Special supervisors, appointed by the Temple, ensured that an adequate number of wells were prepared along the roads, and *mikva'ot* were set up in which the pilgrims could immerse themselves according to biblical law, and thereby arrive in the Holy City in a state of purity.

As the multitudes of pilgrims converged at once to bring their Passover offering to the Holy Temple, special accommodations had to be made which would ensure order. Ovens for roasting the Passover sacrifices were set up

Eating of the first Passover sacrifice, in Egypt, while (opposite) a household member uses a hyssop branch to place some of the blood on the doorposts and lintel of the house, as God commanded.

throughout the city for, after the sacrifice was offered, it would be taken by each family or group and roasted in the special manner prescribed by law to be eaten at the evening *seder*.

A vivid eye-witness account of the vast numbers of pilgrims making their way to Jerusalem from the far-flung corners of the Jewish exile was written by Philo, a leader of

Caravans of pilgrims drawing near to Jerusalem and the Holy Temple, viewed westward from the Mount of Olives. As the pilgrims made their way they sang out, "I was glad when they said unto me, Let us go into the house of the Lord" (Ps. 122:1).

73

the great Jewish community of Alexandria, Egypt, toward the end of the Second Temple era. "Multitudes of people from a multitude of cities flow in an endless stream to the Holy Temple for each festival," he wrote, "from the east and west, from the north and south."

The ceremony of offering the Passover sacrifice was one of the most important events in the calendar of Jerusalem's Holy Temple. Long after its destruction, those who had been privileged to witness it described the huge gates opening and the vast multitudes of joyous celebrants, divided into three groups, streaming into the courtyard, the sound of trumpets and the Levite choir.

The entire people of Israel made the pilgrimage to the Holy Temple on each of the sacred festivals, but more arrived in Jerusalem for Passover than any other time. The Passover sacrifice was incumbent upon both men and women alike, while only the men were obliged to make the offerings in the other festivals. Furthermore, those who did not participate in the Passover offering faced a most severe penalty: the biblical penalty of *karet*, literally, "to be cut off," interpreted by some to mean premature death and by others to indicate a spiritual demotion in the world to come.

To absorb the sudden influx of such a huge number of

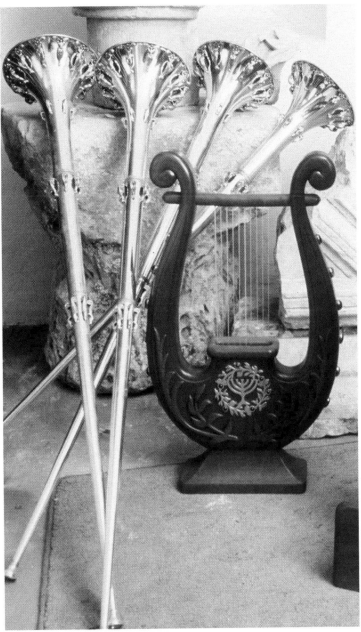

With the Passover sacrifice and matzot *spread before them, a family conducts their* seder, *reclining on cushions and pillows as a sign of freedom.*

Silver trumpets and lyre were among the instruments used by the Levitical choir in the Holy Temple.

(overleaf) As the seder *participants look on, the son poses the "four questions" to his father. At right, attendants carry the roasted Passover sacrifice.*

people, it was necessary to make many technical and logistical arrangements. One was the introduction of many Passover ovens in many locations, to enable everyone to roast the Passover sacrifice after it was offered in the Temple, in preparation for the *seder* later that evening. This sacrifice differed from all those which were brought to the Temple throughout the year, in that the ordinary Israelites who brought them would participate in the preparation of the animal for sacrifice. Although a delegation of Israelites took part in every service, generally speaking only the priests had an active role in the sacrificial service itself. The Passover offering provided one of the few occasions for

Rows of priests standing with silver and gold vessels in their hands, to gather the blood from the sacrifice and to pass the vessels to the priest standing closest to the altar.

When Passover eve fell on the Sabbath, pilgrims would wait with their Passover sacrifice in the courtyard of the Holy Temple. At the conclusion of the Sabbath, all would go their own way to roast the sacrifice in the special ovens prepared throughout Jerusalem for this purpose.

ordinary people to enter the Temple's inner court, where the altar stood.

The Torah requires the Passover sacrifice be eaten in a large communal meal, for gathering as many participants as possible for the Torah brought harmony and a feeling of community to the children of Israel. Moreover, the joy of the Passover celebration was simply not complete unless the poor were present. This was especially true on this holy night, the night of the Exodus, when we celebrate the transition from slavery to freedom.

Each group of pilgrims sent one or two representatives to

the Temple, bringing a lamb as the Passover offering. Once the congregation arrived in the courtyard, the gates were closed and the service was conducted to the sound of the Levites' trumpets. The entire assembly sang the *Hallel* prayers of thanksgiving, led by the Levite choir.

Those standing in the courtyard saw row upon row of priests holding the special silver and gold vessels called *mizrak*, which were used for gathering the blood of the offering. The priest standing closest to the altar received each vessel and poured its contents on the foundation of the altar.

After being offered in the Holy Temple, the Passover sacrifice was roasted by each group or family in one of the special ovens set up all over Jerusalem to accommodate the needs of the festive pilgrims. The sheep or lamb was roasted whole, in keeping with the biblical requirement, on dry pomegranate branches.

After the meal had been prepared, each group reclined at their respective table to conduct the festive Passover *seder*, discussing the miracles of the Exodus, eating *matzot* and bitter herbs dipped in the *haroset* of the *seder* plate and, finally, eating the Passover sacrifice. As midnight approached, the entire household raised their cups for the singing of the *Hallel* prayers of thanksgiving.

The Festival of Shavuot:
Bringing the Firstfruits to the Temple

"The first of the firstfruits of thy land thou shalt bring into the house of the Lord thy God. . ." (Ex. 23:19).

Shavuot is the anniversary of the Revelation of the Law at Mount Sinai. Shavuot, which literally means "weeks," is thus known as the Festival of Weeks because it marked the end of the seven-week period of counting the *omer* which began on the second day of Passover, when the *omer* barley offering was brought to the Temple. Shavuot is also referred to in the Bible as the "feast of firstfruits" (Ex. 23:16; Num. 28:26).

In many ways this festival celebrates the land of Israel itself, when thanks are given to God for His bounty. The bringing of the firstfruit offering to the Holy Temple was a manifestation of the land's intrinsic holiness, given expression through the holiness of the Temple. The Shavuot offering of "firstfruits," which was brought to the Holy Temple and presented to the priest, did not include every species of fruit but only those of the "seven species for which the land of Israel is praised": wheat, barley, grapes, figs, pomegranates, olives, and dates (Deut. 8:8).

Detailed instructions relating to this important occasion are given in Deuteronomy 26: "And it shall be, when thou art come in unto the land which the Lord thy God giveth thee for an inheritance, and possessest it, and dwellest therein; that thou shalt take of the first of all the fruit of the earth, which thou shalt bring of thy land that the Lord thy God giveth thee, and shalt put it in a basket, and shalt go unto the place which the Lord thy God shall choose to place his name there. And thou shalt go unto the priest that shall be in those days, and say unto him, I profess this day unto the Lord thy God, that I am come unto the country which the Lord sware unto our fathers for to give us.

"And the priest shall take the basket out of thine hand, and set it down before the altar of the Lord thy God. And thou shalt speak and say before the Lord thy God, A Syrian ready to perish was my father, and he went down into Egypt, and sojourned there with a few, and became there a nation, great, mighty, and populous: And the Egyptians evil entreated us, and afflicted us, and laid upon us hard bondage: And when we cried unto the Lord God of our fathers, the Lord heard our voice, and looked on our affliction, and our labour, and our oppression:

"And the Lord brought us forth out of Egypt with a mighty hand, and with an outstretched arm, and with great terribleness, and with signs, and with wonders: And he hath brought us into this land, even a land that floweth with milk and honey. And now, behold, I have brought the firstfruits of the land, which thou, O Lord, hast given me. And thou shalt set it before the Lord thy God, and worship before the Lord thy God:

Marking the first fruit by tying a reed around it. The fruit is then brought to the Holy Temple in Jerusalem (opposite).

"And thou shalt rejoice in every good thing which the Lord thy God hath given unto thee, and unto thine house, thou, and the Levite, and the stranger that is among you" (Deut. 26:1–11).

When the fruit began to ripen on the trees, the owner

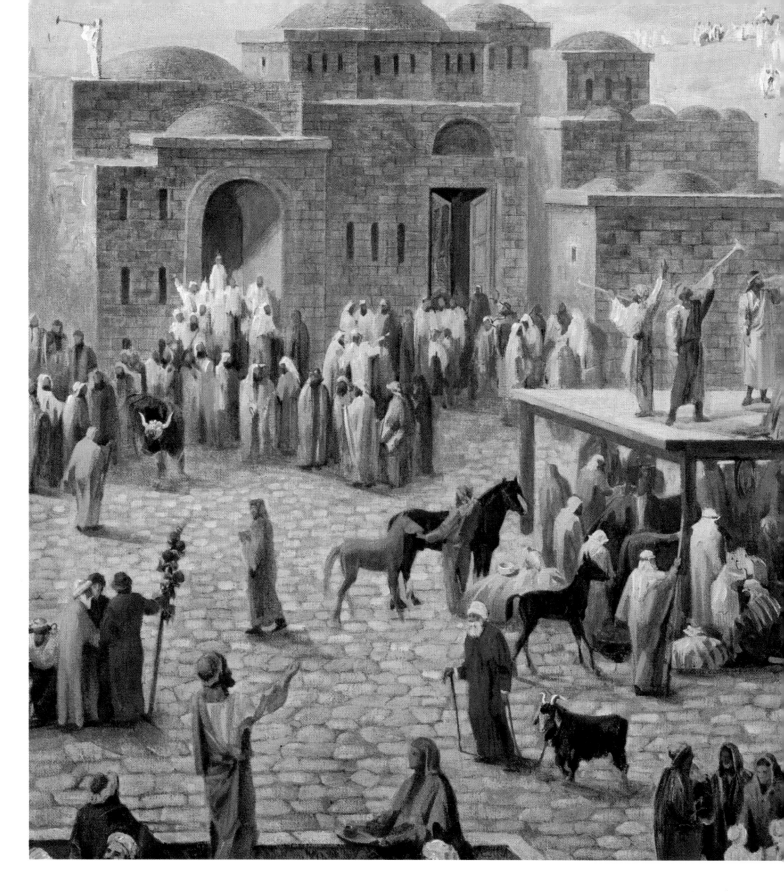

would mark the first by tying a reed around it. Thus he would literally be bringing the *first fruit* of his harvest to the Holy Temple, not just a symbolic representation.

Streams of pilgrims made their way to Jerusalem from towns and villages all over the land. Many families traveled by foot, with the little children in tow; some rode camels and donkeys; and some even rode in wagons and chariots. As they trekked through the gold and green fields ripe with the bountiful harvest, the entire land was literally teeming with excitement and anticipation.

In each district along the route, all the pilgrims from the outlying towns and villages gathered together in the city of the local Assembly Head, who was responsible for the pilgrimage. There, the pilgrims spent the night sleeping in the streets, under the open sky. This was not because of any lack of hospitality but because they did not enter the houses in order to avoid the possibility of becoming exposed to ritual impurity.

They were awakened at dawn, as the first rays of sunlight began to illuminate the sky, by the cry of the overseer: "Arise ye, and let us go up to Zion unto the Lord our God" (Jer. 31:6). They resumed their journey to Jerusalem in a large entourage—for "In the multitude of people is the king's honour" (Prov. 14:28), and as the caravans of

In the town of the Assembly Head, on their way to Jerusalem, the pilgrims spend the night under the open sky, awakened by the cry of "Let us go up to Zion unto the Lord our God."

pilgrims drew near to the Holy Temple, an ox whose horns were overlaid with gold was led before them, the music of flutes accompanied them, and they sang, "I was glad when they said unto me, Let us go into the house of the Lord" (Ps. 122:1). Near the outskirts of the city, a delegation was sent on ahead to the Holy Temple to announce their arrival. All the assistant priests, Levites and the officers of the Temple would go out to greet them, and all the city's tradespeople would cease work to stand and greet them as they entered the gates of the city. As the entourage entered the city, the pilgrims joyously sang, "Our feet shall stand within thy gates, O Jerusalem" (Ps. 122:2).

With their arduous trek behind them, throngs of joyous pilgrims converge on the Eastern Gate of the Temple.

(overleaf) The citizens of Jerusalem greeting the joyous arrival of the festive pilgrims. They lead an ox whose horns are overlaid with gold as the special holiday sacrifice.

By bringing the firstfruits to the Temple, the entire nation expressed heartfelt gratitude for God's bounty; by presenting them to Him, a circle was closed as Nature's yield was returned to its origin. All felt a deep reverence, awe and joy as they acknowledged the Holy One was the source of all blessing. "And thou shalt rejoice in every good thing which the Lord thy God hath given unto thee, and unto thine house . . ." (Deut. 26:11).

Side by side, they stood together and participated in this humbling and gratifying experience—rich and poor alike. "Every man shall give as he is able, according to the blessing of the Lord thy God which he hath given thee" (Deut. 16:17).

The ceremony of bringing the firstfruit offering was held in a special area within the Holy Temple, a section designated as "between the hall and the altar." This area had a special sanctity, and entrance therein was forbidden to ordinary Israelites. However, the commandment of the firstfruit offering differed from all other sacrifices in that an ordinary Israelite was not only permitted, but actually *commanded* to fulfill this Divine obligation in that very place.

Presenting his offering to the priests, each pilgrim would read aloud from the biblical portion of "My father was a

homeless Aramean" (Deut. 26:5). The officiating priest recited each verse aloud in Hebrew, and the pilgrim repeated it after him. The pilgrim had lowered the basket from his shoulder, holding it by the rim or by its handles while the officiating priest stood opposite him, placed his own hands underneath the basket, and "waved" it before God. Once the pilgrim had completed the recitation of the biblical verses, he would set down his basket of firstfruits in the court, as the verse states: "And thou shalt set it before the Lord thy God" (ibid. v. 10). The basket was placed on the southwestern corner of the altar, and the bearer concluded the ceremony by prostrating himself "before

Facing the direction of the Holy of Holies, festive pilgrims fully prostrate themselves as a sign of reverence and awe for the Divine Presence.

(above) The golden flask used to carry water from the Siloam spring up to the Holy Temple for the Festival of the Water Libation during Tabernacles.

(right) Priests pouring the wine and water libations into two silver cups that were set into the southwestern corner of the altar.

the Lord," hands and feet spread out, opposite the stairs leading up to the Sanctuary's entrance. A special stone was used especially for this purpose in the Holy Temple.

In addition to the firstfruit offering of the seven species, another offering was brought to the Temple on Shavuot, the "twin loaves" baked from the newly harvested wheat. This, the only leaven ever brought to the Temple, represented God's blessing on man's earthly, physical needs throughout the year. These two loaves were waved on the eastern side of the altar by a priest, together with an

offering of two sheep for the festival. Each loaf had been formed into brick-like shapes, measuring seven handbreadths long and four handbreadths wide (each "handbreadth" measured approximately eight centimeters), and four fingers high (the measurement of a "finger" was about two centimeters).

When the time for the wine libation and offering of the twin loaves arrived, the Levites accompanied the ceremony with singing, and the playing of flutes and trumpets: "Also in the days of your gladness, and in your solemn days . . . ye shall blow with the trumpets . . ." (Num. 10:10).

On the eastern side of the altar, the officiating priest would "wave" the two sacrificial sheep. Then the priests would partake of the "twin loaves" together with the remaining meat from the congregational peace offerings.

It would appear that this meal could not have been eaten within the court proper, since that area was filled to capacity with the holiday pilgrims. It is probable that the priests partook of the twin loaves in the Place of Fire, within the sanctified section which opened onto the court.

The Priestly and Levitical Watches

The tribe of Levi was completely separated and charged with the service of the Holy Temple: "At that time the Lord separated the tribe of Levi, to bear the ark of the covenant of the Lord, to stand before the Lord to minister unto him, and to bless in his name, unto this day. Wherefore Levi hath no part nor inheritance with his brethren, according as the Lord thy God promised him" (Deut. 10:8–9).

The Levites were commanded to be available and to be prepared to carry out the service of the Temple, unoccupied with other pursuits. Their tasks included guarding the Temple, opening the doors at the start of the daily service, and locking them at the close of the day: "And they [the Levites] shall be joined unto thee, and keep the charge of the tabernacle of the congregation, for all the service of the tabernacle . . ." (Num. 18:4). Altogether, watches were kept in 24 locations throughout the Holy Temple. The majority of these—21—were manned by the Levites, and three by priests. The three locations where the priests stood watch were the Chamber of Avtinas, the Chamber of the Spark, and the Place of Fire. Unlike ordinary guard stations or "checkpoints," these watches were not for the purpose of guarding against intruders, but rather to glorify the honor and dignity of the House of God.

The first two watch stations were structures built into the side of the court like upper lofts. In the Chamber of Avtinas the incense which was offered up on the golden incense altar in the Sanctuary was prepared; it was named after the priestly Avtinas family who were entrusted with the sacred task of compounding the ingredients and creating the incense for the service. This chamber was located on the south side of the court, directly over the "Water Gate" (so called because it was through this gate that the golden flask of water was brought up to the Temple from the Siloam spring on Sukkot, during the Festival of the Water Libation).

The Chamber of the Spark was located in the north of the court. Here, a small fire was kept burning to provide flame for the fire which burned perpetually atop the altar. The watches in both the Chamber of Avtinas and the Chamber of the Spark were manned by young priests who had not yet reached the age of their official Temple duties.

The Place of Fire was also situated on the northern side, east of the Chamber of the Spark. This was not an upper loft, however, but a very large room covered with a domed roof. A large fire was kept burning here all the time, where the officiating shifts of priests could warm themselves on

their return from immersing themselves for purification.

The Place of Fire was also the priests' dormitory. Whichever family division would be reponsible for the next day's service would sleep in this room the night before. Some would sleep on the floor and some on specially

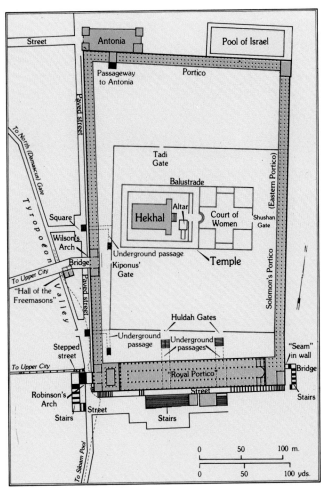

Plan of the Temple Mount during the Second Temple period.

constructed "bunk beds," wide slabs of cut stone that were built into the walls of this room like steps. The elders, being more sensitive, would sleep on these stone slabs while the younger priests slept on the floor.

The Levites also guarded an additional 21 stations. Five

groups of Levites stood guard at the five gates leading into the Temple Mount:

The double "Huldah Gates" on the southern side of the Temple Mount were named after Huldah the prophetess (see 2 Kings 22:14), who sat between them during the days of the First Temple, and told her prophecies to the people entering and leaving the Temple. These two gates served as the main entrance and exit for the Temple Mount. Since the majority of the buildings and activities were on the southern side of the complex, most of the traffic was through this side, and therefore two gates were necessary to accommodate the flow of people.

The "Kiponus" Gate on the western side was probably named after the benefactor who contributed the funds for its construction, although some authorities maintain that the word is derived from the Greek for "garden work," and that a rose garden was located in the proximity of this gate.

This gate also facilitated entrance and exit.

The "Tadi" Gate on the north, unlike the others, was not used for gaining access to and from the Temple. According to some scholars, it was built exclusively for decorative purposes but others maintain that a priest who had inadvertently become defiled (and, thus, would have to cease his service, and leave the holy areas of the Temple in order to purify himself by immersion) would leave unobtrusively through the Tadi Gate (as indicated by the Aramaic translation of the word, which carries a connotation of "modesty" or "secret").

The "Eastern," or Shushan Gate, located on the eastern side of the Temple Mount, featured a massive illustration of Shushan (Susa), capital of ancient Persia, and had been created in honor of the Persian kingdom that ruled in the land of Israel during the first days of the Second Temple and had given permission for its rebuilding. It was through

this gate that the High Priest would escort the red heifer and the entire entourage of priests and assistants to the Mount of Anointment (the Mount of Olives) to the place where it was burned for the process of ritual purification.

Four shifts of Levites also stood guard at the four inner corners of the Temple Mount wall. Another five shifts watched at the five gates to the court, while another four guarded the four outside corners of the Temple Mount.

The remaining three watch stations consisted of one shift in the Chamber of Sacrifices, one in the Chamber of the Curtain and one behind the Holy of Holies. The Chamber of Lambs was one of four small chambers located within the four corners of the Place of Fire. It was in the southwest corner, and in it were lambs which were free from blemishes and had been chosen for the daily sacrifices. The Chamber of the Curtain was used by those who weaved the curtains in the Temple. Its exact location is unknown.

A reconstruction of the Temple Mount during the Second Temple period, based on archaeological and historical evidence.

The Daily Song of the Levitical Choir

Each day, the Levitical choir (opposite) stood atop the platform located in the Court of Israel facing the outer altar, just inside the Nikanor Gates, and sang the song for that particular day. On the festivals and New Moon, however, different songs were sung. All were performed together with their instrumental arrangements, while the morning and evening wine libations were poured onto the altar by the officiating priests. Thus the Levites complemented the Divine service of the priests with a service of their own and, in many ways, the Levitical songs were as important a Temple function as the priestly service of the sacrifices itself, for the one could not function without the other. At three points in their song, the Levites would pause, the priests would sound the silver trumpets and all the people in the court would prostrate themselves before the presence of God.

The order of the daily songs has a deep significance, and there is a mystical connection which each song had for the particular day it was sung. On Sunday, the first day of the week, they sang Psalm 24, which begins "The earth is the Lord's, and the fulness thereof," for Sunday is the first day of creation.

On Monday, they sang Psalm 48, which begins "Great is the Lord, and greatly to be praised in the city of our God, in the mountain of his holiness." It was on this day that the waters were divided, and God made the firmament between the upper and lower waters (Gen. 1:6–7).

On Tuesday, the Levites sang Psalm 82, which begins "God standeth in the congregation of the mighty; he judgeth among the gods," for on this day of creation the dry land became visible and it is upon this land that the judges stand to render their decisions.

On Wednesday, they sang Psalm 94, which begins "O Lord God, to whom vengeance belongeth; O God, to whom vengeance belongeth, shew thyself." This was the day wherein the sun, moon and stars were created and, in the future, He will excercise judgment and exact vengeance from those idolators who worship these heavenly bodies, as if they themselves were gods.

On Thursday, they sang Psalm 81, which begins "Sing aloud unto God our strength: make a joyful noise unto the God of Jacob." The living creatures were created on this day, and when we perceive the myriad variations and diversity of God's handiwork, we are filled with awe and wonder and give praise to their Creator.

On Friday, the Levites sang Psalm 93, which begins "The Lord reigneth, he is clothed with majesty," for the creation was crowned and completed on this day. On the sixth day, man was created, and only he can recognize God's true greatness. Man alone has the capacity to understand the Creator's dominion and accept His sovereignty.

Playing the trumpets, with Mount Moriah and the Holy Temple in the background.

On the holy Sabbath, the Levites sang Psalm 92, "A Psalm or Song for the Sabbath day." The sages of Israel taught that this psalm was a song for the future, perfected world, "the day which is complete Sabbath tranquillity, for everlasting life."

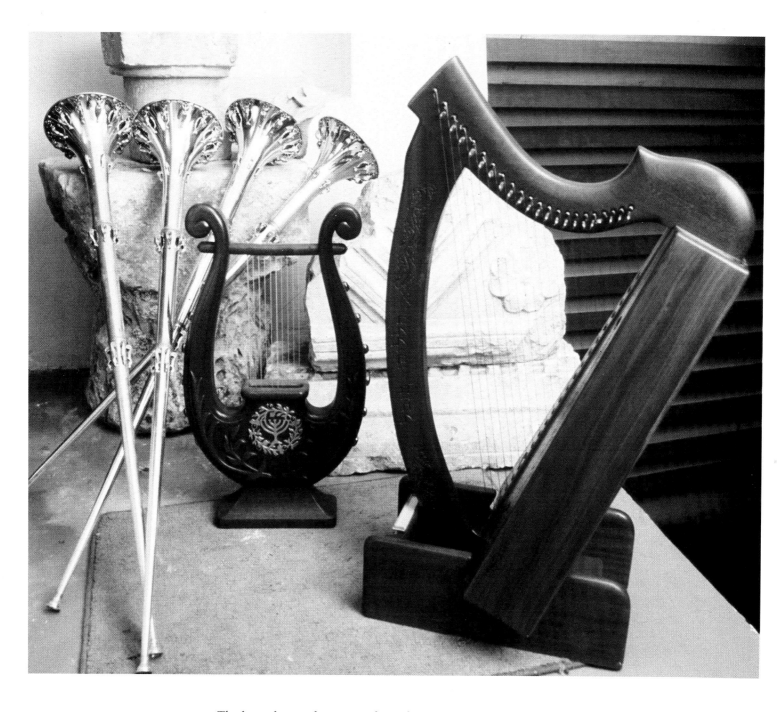

The harp, lyre and trumpets figured prominently in the daily song sung by the Levites in the Holy Temple.